EDVARD MUNCH
Close-Up of a Genius

Rolf E. Stenersen

EDVARD MUNCH

Close-Up of a Genius

Translated and Edited by
Reidar Dittmann

Publisher
Sem & Stenersen A/S
OSLO

Edvard Munch. Close-Up of a Genius
First published in Stockholm 1944
First Norwegian edition, Oslo 1945
First English edition, Oslo 1969
5th edition, Oslo 2001
Copyright © Sem & Stenersen A/S
Photoset, printed: PDC Tangen
Printed in Norway 2001
ISBN 82-7046-057-5

The illustrations have generously been made available
by Munch-museet, Oslo.

Front cover:
Self-Portrait with Cigarette, 1895
110 x 85.5 cm, Nasjonalgalleriet, Oslo

Back cover:
Portrait of Rolf Stenersen, 1925
110 x 90 cm, Munch-museet, Oslo

Contents

Home and Family

Handsome men sometimes appear effeminate and weak. Edvard Munch was handsome and of a delicate nature. Nevertheless, his appearance revealed neither effeminacy nor weakness. He had an unusually strong and beautiful head. People passing him in the street would turn around and follow him with their eyes—long before he became a famous artist. To see Edvard Munch was an unforgettable experience.

His hair was blond and wavy, his forehead arched and high, his eyes bluish gray. His nose and mouth were attractively shaped, despite a somewhat narrow lower lip, and, because he always carried his head high, his strong chin gave an illusion of great strength.

He was slender, a little taller than average, erect but not athletic. As soon as his financial condition allowed it, he had all his clothes made by the best tailors. Even so, he never quite managed to look well dressed. His total appearance, however—his straight back, his chiseled features—gave an impression of ancient nobility.

Pola Gauguin, in his biography of Munch, has called attention to the facial similarity between the Norwegian artist and Leonardo da Vinci. Munch's forehead was higher and his upper lip stronger than Leonardo's, otherwise the resemblance is remarkable. They also possessed many similar personality traits. Strong-willed, they were both of such hypersensitive emotional fiber that they remained strangers on earth, unable to keep in step with anyone else—and neither was capable of sharing his life with a woman.

Edvard Munch's handsome appearance alone did not

fully account for the curiosity of passers-by. Other features commanded attention. He seemed odd. His eyes, dreamy and remote, counteracted the effect of his determined chin. His hands were small, and his arms, extending limply from narrow shoulders, seemed totally devoid of strength. He walked erratically—would stop now and then to ponder something, take a few steps again, then turn as if to change direction. Invariably, however, he would revert to his original course and continue slowly on his way—usually walking close to the buildings.

On his father's side, Edvard Munch belonged to one of Norway's most distinguished cultural families. In his lineage were artists and scholars, among them the historian Peter Andreas Munch, Edvard's uncle, whose works were of basic importance during the nation's nineteenth century quest for cultural independence; and Andreas Munch, popular poet and playwright of the national romantic period. On his mother's side, he hailed from a long line of farmers, sea captains, and merchants.

Edvard Munch's father, Christian, was a physician. By nature a dreamer, he had in his youth sailed far and wide as a shipboard doctor and loved to spin long tales about these adventurous journeys. In his mid-forties he married Laura Bjølstad, twenty years his junior, the daughter of a merchant in the Oslofjord city of Fredrikstad. Five children had been born to the family when the mother succumbed to tuberculosis at the age of thirty-three.

Edvard, the second child, born December 12, 1863, was only five years old when his mother passed away. Her tragically premature death cast a deep and lasting shadow on the family. The father, whose lighthearted stories had amused and entertained the children, now turned to the Bible for comfort and became a withdrawn religious brooder. Influenced by biblical demands, he refused to accept payment from patients he considered poor, and the Munchs began to experience serious financial difficulties.

The family was ridden with illness. Eight years after the mother's death, the oldest daughter, Sofie, died—also from tuberculosis. Records of the family's past told of mental disturbances, and the second oldest daughter, very alert in her early school years, later suffered from insanity and ultimately died in a mental institution.

A year after Laura Munch's death, her youngest sister, Karen Bjølstad, took over the household duties. An able housekeeper and very good with the children, she became a great comfort to the hypersensitive Edvard. The oldest of the boys—and after his sister's death also the oldest of the children—he ran into frequent conflicts with his father whom he both loved and feared; but with his young aunt he soon established a warm friendship which grew deeper during Sofie's lingering illness. His sister's tragedy weighed heavily on his thirteen-year-old shoulders, and it had an almost shocking effect on him that his father, a physician, was unable to save her, and that the entire family's fervent prayers were of no avail.

His aunt painted a little in her spare time—often pasting leaves, twigs, and moss into her paintings. Edvard was inspired and it was not long before he became as eager a painter as she was. Thus, his first artistic help and guidance he received from his young aunt whom he came to love with a fervor far greater than he dared show.

In his childhood, Edvard Munch was often bedridden, mostly with bronchitis, but three times also with rheumatic fever. These frequent and lengthy illnesses ruined his schooling. His best subject had always been arithmetic, a field in which Doctor Munch had hoped his son would go far. A great task, the doctor thought, was to harness Norway's mighty supply of water power, and he liked to envision his son playing an important part in this national development. Nothing came of it—first, because Edvard was no great success in school, and secondly because he wanted to become an artist, an occupational choice Doctor Munch could not possibly approve of. To be an artist, he said, was like living in a brothel.

"But can't you see the boy has talent?" Karen Bjølstad asked. "I tell you, Edvard's drawings are really remarkable."

So he was allowed to attend the municipal art school. Through the intervention of his aunt, he could now plan to become a painter, the only occupation for which he felt suited. No one ever did more for him.

Edvard, however, despite this and all her other kindnesses, sometimes felt deceived by her, as when she happened to take his father's side in family arguments. Then he strongly suspected that she had plans of becoming something more important in the household than sister-in-law and housekeeper. Yet when Doctor Munch actually did propose marriage to her she replied: "No. I don't want to become a step-mother."

In these early years, when Edvard made numerous pictures of all those in the household, he rarely portrayed his aunt. When he does include her in a composition he makes her sit with head bowed or face completely hidden, as if he has not wanted to look her in the eyes.

In 1884, when he was twenty-one and she forty-four, he painted a strange picture of her. She is seated in a rocking chair, eyes fixed on the floor, portrayed as a young woman, not much older than the artist. Dressed in dark, she reflects an aura of wonderment and secrecy. Her soft lines have been suggested in a series of small, vibrant spots of light, like caresses. Even into her ear, on the shadowy side of the composition, he has eased a spot of light.

Very many of Edvard Munch's best pictures are based on specific reminiscences from his childhood and early youth. In *Sick Girl* and *Springtime,* he has brought back the memory of his aunt watching over his ailing sister. When he painted these works his actual models were strangers. Even so, the figures he has wanted to portray are those of his aunt and his sister.

A story he once told concerning an episode between himself and his father indicates that his persistent tendency to dodge difficulties by escaping into his art was an early personality trait.

"I happened to argue with my father one evening regarding the duration of the unbeliever's agony in hell," he recalled. "As I saw it, no sin was so great that God would extend the agony beyond a thousand years. But father saw it differently and claimed that the torment would last a thousand times a thousand years. I refused to give in and finally stalked out in a huff slamming the door behind me. Of course, it didn't take me long to walk off my anger, and I soon returned home to put things right with father. When I got there he had gone to his bedroom. From the door which I had opened quietly I saw him kneeling by his bed, something I had never seen him do before. I closed the door gently and went to my own room. There, restless and unable to sleep, I brought out my sketch book and started to draw. I drew my father kneeling by his bed. The soft light on the night-stand cast a yellow glow over his night shirt. I filled in the colors. As soon as it was finished I went to bed and slept soundly."

Money was a scarce item in the Munch household. Thus, when Inger, Edvard's younger sister, informed the family that her best friend's father had promised to buy one of Edvard's paintings, she was met with a mixture of enthusiasm and doubt. The prospective buyer, a contractor who had suddenly done well, felt the need of a painting above his desk, and, actually knowing no other painter than young Edvard, had informed Inger that he planned to call on her family on Sunday to make the necessary arrangements.

"Did he make a definite promise to that effect?" the doctor wanted to know, and, "do you think he has that much money?"

"Of course, he promised," Inger replied indignantly; "and everyone can see he has a lot of money. After all, his two daughters, both younger than me, have been given sealskin muffs quite recently. They're probably on the way now." She went to the window and scanned the street below.

"By the way, Edvard, have you finished any of your pictures?" Doctor Munch asked. "It isn't right to sell an unfinished picture, you know."

Inger had remained by the window. "There they are!" she exclaimed as she peered out into the semi-darkness.

Edvard went over and looked out the window too. Thinking he saw some sealskin muffs below, he went into his room to give a couple of pictures a hurried finishing touch. A moment later he was back in the living room asking his father's advice regarding the price.

"What should I charge him, father?"

"That ought to be your own decision, my boy."

"Couldn't you stay and talk to the contractor," Edvard pleaded. "I really have to go out for a while."

"No, this is for you to take care of. You must get used to selling your own pictures. Besides"—he looked from his son to the pictures—"I'm not sure you have quite finished them." Scanning the canvases with a critical eye, he added wistfully: "Wouldn't you rather want to amount to something, Edvard? Imagine all the waterfalls we have in this country."

Doctor Munch left. Edvard remained home with his aunt and the rest of the family. He found it difficult to sit still—moved restlessly from one chair to another. But the contractor and his daughters never showed up, and when Doctor Munch returned Edvard had gone to bed. The father went quietly into his son's room and said gently: "Edvard, the most difficult thing in this world is to sell a picture."

Early Years

As a young man, Edvard Munch joined a circle of artists and intellectuals who met regularly in the restaurant of Oslo's Grand Hotel. Mentor of this Bohemian group was Hans Jaeger, a writer of local fame, who earned his daily bread as parliament clerk. His two-volume work *From the Life of the Oslo Boheme,* an unusually honest and outspoken novel, was promptly confiscated by the authorities and its author sentenced to a prison term for blasphemy and indecency. In his programmatic work, published in 1906 and titled *The Bible of the Anarchy,* Jaeger leads all evil back to Christianity, whose moral demands, he claims, repress man's vital desires and functions, principally his sexual drive. This human function, far from being merely a simple mating process, is a source of pleasure, a wave of sweetness and warmth, through which man is elevated and made less lonely. Christianity, however, with its strict moral demands, makes man hard, cold, and false. Honesty and openness are man's greatest virtues, while bourgeois morality, most flagrantly demonstrated in the standard marriage, is a pillar of hypocrisy.

Munch, only a lukewarm member of this rather noisy group of intellectuals, found it easier to share their enthusiasm in theory than in practice, and it is significant to note that the one person in the group with whom he was able to form a close bond of friendship was Sigbjørn Obstfelder, a timid but talented lyric poet whose significant contribution to the Norwegian literature did not become fully recognized until after his premature death. Obstfelder craved Munch's company and often humbly asked permission to be with him. On such occasions the two might sit for long periods of time in complete silence. One day Obstfelder declared: "It's so good to sit here by you, Edvard. Really, I can't stand to be with the others."

Poverty created a bond between all these struggling artists. When one of them was hungry and penniless, he would seek out the others at the Grand Restaurant to find someone able to provide food and a drink, the latter being more readily available.

To this lively circle belonged also a few ladies of the bourgeoisie who had accepted the idea that the relationship between man and woman should be free, simple, and direct. Those attracted to each other, they felt, would simply live together until one or both of the parties decided to terminate the union. It did not take long before difficulties arose.

"Sooner or later one of our ladies would get all excited," Munch recalled, "and start screaming at the top of her voice, •'Oh God, I'm pregnant, I'm pregnant! You've got to marry me!'"

One of these ladies fell in love with Edvard Munch. The daughter of a rich businessman, she was much more fond of artists than of art. Munch was with her quite often but had no intention of becoming tied down.

"She was the type of woman I always run into—with a long pointed nose and thin, narrow lips—actually a type I don't care for at all. As soon as I had settled down to paint, she'd call me up and ask me to meet her.

"'Come on down, Edvard,' she would plead. 'It's so nice here. You can always paint tomorrow.'

"Well, to put an end to it, I decided to take a boat to a remote village a few hours to the south to be able to work in peace. But wouldn't you know it, she sent a mutual friend down there? I had to come back, he said. She had shot herself and lay dying, calling my name all the time. Really, there was no time to waste.

"But no sooner had I arrived in her room than she jumped up from her bed shouting jubilantly: 'You see, Edvard, you do love me, don't you! I knew you'd come!'

"We quarreled, and she actually pulled out a gun, threatening: 'Now I'm really going to kill myself.' I didn't believe she'd do it, you know, but just to be gallant I put my hand over hers. And she actually pulled the trigger and shot off a part of my finger. Do you know what she said when she saw the bleeding wound? 'I didn't mean to do it, Edvard,' she said. 'I hope it doesn't hurt!'

"And when I left she ran after me down the steps shouting all the time: 'Edvard, I love you, I love you!'"

It certainly did hurt. In fact, Edvard Munch never quite got over it. To hide his maimed finger he always wore gloves and inside his left glove a large ring on the same finger.

Having experienced difficulties with people before, he now became more withdrawn than ever. If in bitterness and depravity a person would go so far as to shoot off a painter's finger, Munch reasoned, he could no longer expose himself to society. Then it was far better to stay home and paint. If people wanted to know what he thought of them and their habits all they'd have to do would be to have a look at his pictures. They might have found his works wanting in warmth and happiness, but only because what other people dreamed of and yearned for in life were unknown to him. To him life, a constant quest for a non-existent happiness, was nothing but turmoil and need, sex, sorrow, and anguish. The only possible source of anything divine was the sun and the light.

He was twenty-three years old when he created the canvases which first focused attention on his talent—*Sick Girl, The Day After,* and *Puberty.*

Sick Girl, representing a great deal more than the painter's farewell to a beloved sister, is really a poem, a vision of death. A young girl sits feebly in a chair, her eyes turned toward the light. Ennobled by death, her wan face, merging imperceptibly with the daylight which floods the room, is framed by soft reddish hair and marked by a gentle spot of red near the mouth. The aunt, sitting at the girl's side, bows her head. The very moment we view the picture the struggle is over—the girl's eyes are transfixed. The figure and the light become one.

The painting is held in muted tones of gray and green. The lines, sketched in with great tenderness, are felt rather than seen, and the entire canvas exudes a spirit of peace and deliverance.

With this picture, Munch released an artistic avalanche. Here, for once, were not only colors and lines. This was music—it was poetry and yearning. From dust hast thou come, to *light* shalt thou be ...

The Day After shows a half-dressed, deathly weary woman in drunken stupor on a bed. On the night-stand are bottles and glasses. Her blouse is unbuttoned, one arm and her hair tossed in our direction—now she can sleep.

In *Puberty,* a nude adolescent girl is sitting on the edge of a bed, a huge, sack-like shadow—the phallic symbol—hovers ominously in the background. Shyly covering herself with her crossed hands, she squeezes one of these tightly between her knees, and we sense in the white figure the advent of sex and anxiety.

That the reception given Munch at the first showing of these pictures consisted primarily of abuse and sarcasm was, perhaps, not surprising. The critics, morally shaken, found the pictures sickly and brutal. In Oslo's principal newspaper, one wrote:

"Edvard Munch is best served by having his pictures bypassed in silence. With these paintings, the level of the entire exhibit has been lowered. By accepting them, the jury has done the artist a disfavor."

Said another: "For Munch's own sake I do wish that his *Sick Girl* had been rejected. Not because it speaks less clearly of his talent than do his earlier pictures, but because it shows that he does not take his own artistic development seriously. As it now appears, the study is a worthless, half erased sketch, an abortive attempt."

And a third: "Here is no longer a question of nature, only bizarre madness, delirious moods, and feverish hallucinations."

16

Even Munch's own cousin, the painter Gustav Wentzel, a naturalist, bemoaned the technique: "You paint like a pig, Edvard. That's no way to paint hands. They look more like sledge-hammers."

"We can't all paint branches and fingernails," Munch replied sullenly.

A fellow painter happened to comment favorably on *Sick Girl,* and Munch promptly gave the picture to him. Thirty years later, another version brought more than ten thousand dollars.

When the National Gallery in Oslo purchased *The Day After* one of the city's most prominent critics lamented: "Now our citizens can no longer bring their daughters to the Gallery. How long will Munch's drunken prostitute be allowed to sleep it off in the state's own art center?"

Of one of his most outspoken critics Munch said: "When he failed as a poet and his eyes became diseased he turned to art criticism."

In art circles, many realized early that Edvard Munch was a great painter—a new mirror of the age. Among those in Oslo who gave him their unqualified support were Christian Krohg and Erik Werenskiold.

Christian Krohg, leading exponent of naturalism in Norway, a skilled artist and teacher and an effective and uncompromising writer, contributed significantly to the development of Norwegian art. It was he who, having commented favorably on *Sick Girl,* suddenly found himself the owner of the controversial canvas.

Erik Werenskiold, although initially subscribing faithfully to the naturalistic tendencies of the 1880's, developed a deep reverence for the national romantic element and became Norway's principal interpreter of folklore, painting landscapes of deeply lyric quality and creating masterful pen and ink illustrations for a series of popular editions of works from the national literary treasure—the sagas and the folk tales. Although Munch was far from charitable in his evaluation of the works of Krohg and Werenskiold, these two championed his cause and assisted him with gifts and other kinds of support in his days of need.

Munch's first trip abroad took place in 1885 when he went to Paris for a three weeks' stay. Four years later, when he was twenty-six and received a state stipend, he returned to Paris and studied for four months with Bonnat. Equally important, perhaps, was his exposure to paintings by Manet, Pissarro, Seurat, Signac, and Couture.

The state allowed him additional grants, and in subsequent years he traveled a great deal—to France, Germany, and Italy. Yet almost every year, with the coming of spring, he returned to his beloved Oslofjord region.

In his early career, Munch lived rather recklessly.

"I don't remember much of Paris," he said once in a reminiscent mood; "we used to have a few drinks before breakfast just to sober up; later we drank to get back into a stupor.

"Train personnel are pleasant people," he mused. "They have seen and heard quite a bit, you know, and can give valuable advice to a passenger who needs it. Once in those early years I was going back to Norway from Germany—didn't have a ticket so I spent most of my time en route hiding out in the washroom. But the conductor found me anyway. I told him I was a Norwegian and that I had run out of money. 'Why didn't you go to the legation and ask to be sent home?' he queried. 'They'd have given you some money. Here, have a sausage!'"

Once, having spent some time in Nice, Munch proceeded to Monte Carlo where he ran into some Norwegian friends who thought they had developed an infallible method to beat the roulette wheel. Every time one color came up in five consecutive games, they would bet a few francs on another color. If they lost they simply doubled the stakes. Playing that way for a few days, they had made a little more than their daily need. At first, Munch had little confidence in the method, but when he saw with his own eyes that it seemed to work, he decided to give it a try. He wanted to start with one hundred francs and increase the bet each time he won.

"The most difficult problem," he said, "was to decide on the amount that would constitute reasonable winnings. I told myself: Edvard, how much do you need to be able to paint *whenever* and *however* you want? I came to the conclusion that fifty thousand francs was the minimum. So I thought I'd go to sixty thousand to have an additional ten thousand to give to someone else in need. I promised myself I would quit as soon as I had reached sixty thousand and was absolutely certain I would not be caught by greediness and gambling mania. As soon as I had won the required amount I would get up calmly and walk out. So I took a seat by a table where black and red seem to come up alternately. I sat there for a long time waiting for *one* color to win five consecutive times. That would be my cue. But the exchange between black and red continued. I found the croupier suspicious and moved to another table. That croupier was not to my liking either, but I stayed on long enough to see black come up for the fifth consecutive time. Very deliberately I placed one hundred francs on red. Black again. I doubled my bet, staying with red. Would you believe it? Black came up for the seventh time, and the suspicious-looking croupier shoveled my money in, shoveled it into his corner with a long stick. It went so fast, I thought—there it was, and then it was gone. Well, I left the room and went out into the garden to eat a few sandwiches I had in a package. Later I went into a *pissoir*. Suddenly, an attendant entered and implored me not to commit suicide.

"'Suicide?' I said. 'I'm a painter and I haven't the slightest intention of committing suicide.'

"'You can have a ticket to Nice and twenty francs extra if you promise to leave.'

"He accompanied me to the station and I went back to Nice. I'm no gambler. All I wanted was some money."

The Berlin Period and The Frieze of Life

"You have become famous by creating an uproar," the Danish poet Holger Drachmann said to Munch as they sat with August Strindberg, the Swedish dramatist, in the Berlin tavern *Zum schwarzen Ferkel* one evening. Munch got up and left.

"Is it news to you that great art usually creates an uproar?" Strindberg asked Drachmann.

It was 1892. Munch, having been invited by the Union of Berlin Artists to take part in its November Exhibit, arrived in the German capital with fifty-five canvases. No sooner had the formal opening of the exhibit taken place than some of the Union's leading members demanded that it be closed—"in the name of Art and honest artistic work."

The German press printed stories of an insane Norwegian artist who had been asked to exhibit in Berlin. Although because of the Munch paintings the exhibit actually was closed, many of Germany's younger artists, with Max Liebermann as their spokesman, came to Munch's defence and appealed the decision of the Union. A violent polemic ensued in the course of which Edvard Munch's fame grew. Newspapers and magazines wrote about him. Having been bawled out in one of Europe's principal cities, he had become a sensational subject.

Initially, his art appealed only to a few, but his circle of supporters increased rapidly. Young poets were particularly eager to point to him in their writings.

Already in 1894—when Munch was 31 years old—the Germans published books about him. "I have never paid anyone a penny to write about me," he said, "but to some writers I gave piles of graphic works."

In Berlin in the 1890's, Munch met a person who contributed much to his success: the art patron Albert Kollmann, and, through him, other wealthy men who were to become mentors of his art, Dr. Max Linde, Count Harry Kessler, Dr. Herbert Esche, and Bruno and Paul Cassirer, the art dealers. Through Kessler, Munch met Mrs. Förster-Nietzsche, whom he painted while she talked incessantly about her famous brother; and Munch painted him also—from a photograph.

After long conversations with Albert Kollmann, who believed in mysterious forces, Munch began to consider his main work—*The Frieze of Life*. Many of his principal canvases—also those completed earlier—would eventually be woven into this frieze which would consist of a series of paintings intended to give a comprehensive view of man's struggle, his difficulties and joys—his total inner being.

Munch soon tired of Kollmann, packed his suitcase in secret, and rushed to the train station to escape. The moment he was to step onto the train, however, Kollmann suddenly stood before him, speaking very calmly and matter-of-factly:

"You've got to finish that frieze of pictures before I can let you go."

"Frankly, I don't understand how Kollmann could have known exactly where I was," Munch said later when he talked about this episode. "There must be something to Strindberg's idea of waves that surround us and affect us. Perhaps we have a sort of receiver in our brain. I often turn back when I walk in the street—feel that if I continue I'll meet someone or other whom I don't like. I can't stand the feeling that someone gets a hold on me. Even so, I did let this Faustian Kollmann order me around. We returned to his home, and I continued working on *The Frieze of Life*." On a brighter note, he added: "I must admit that Kollmann had a peculiar talent for coming across with five hundred marks at the exact moments when my money had run out."

Munch has written this explanation of *The Frieze of Life:*

"*The Frieze of Life* is conceived as a sequence of pictures which together might give a picture of life itself. Through it the undulating shoreline twines and twists—beyond it is the sea in constant motion. Under the crests of the trees, life in all its fullness unfolds its sorrows and joys. The frieze is intended to be a poem of life, of love and death. The theme of the largest painting—*Man and Woman in the Forest*—may appear to be somewhat in the periphery of the central idea, but it is an equally necessary link in the total chain—the buckle, in fact, which ties the belt together. This painting of the nude man and woman in the forest—the city dimly visible in the distance—is a picture of life and death; the forest drawing life from the dead, the city emerging behind the crests of the trees. It is a picture of the strong, sustaining forces of life."

One of the central paintings in the frieze is *The Dance of Life.* Under the full moon young people are dancing near a shore caressed by the waves. The figures are encircled by an aura of colors to which the moon adds an intense, phosphorescent glow. Flames of brown and red, emanating from the ground, blend with shades of dark-green which seep in from the woods. Each detail contributes to the aura which surrounds and affects all and binds the individual elements together into a meaningful totality.

While working on *The Frieze of Life,* Munch received his first commission. Dr. Max Linde offered him 4,000 marks and free accommodation in return for wall decorations in his children's room. For the first time in his life, Munch had favorable working conditions. He went to Dr. Linde's home—and continued to concentrate on the frieze. When he handed the pictures to Dr. Linde, Munch's host refused to accept them. After all, the frieze was not exactly what he had envisioned for his children's room. Thirty years later, when offered one million *kroner* for these pictures, Munch refused to sell. Instead of *The Frieze of Life,* Munch handed Dr. Linde portraits he had painted of everyone in the household and a folder containing etchings of the Linde property.

Next, Munch was commissioned to paint stage sets for Max Reinhardt's theatre. Even then, he actually continued painting on *The Frieze of Life* and in the work for Max Reinhardt added many new pictures to the series. These, held in restrained, muted colors, give the effect of a glimpse into a world of dreams.

Another German who took an early liking to Munch was Dr. Herbert Esche, who invited the painter to stay in his house; Munch reciprocated by painting Dr. Esche and his children. On occasion, in those days of revelry, matters might easily get out of hand. One evening, in a tavern not far from the Esche house, Munch lifted his glass and shouted: "Free drinks for all. Doctor Esche pays!"

When the bill reached 110 marks, the apprehensive tavern operator called Dr. Esche who said: "All right, you will get your 110 marks—on the condition that you get Munch back to the house."

After a few glasses Edvard Munch was anything but quiet and shy in the early days. Then, seething with life, he was often quite bold. On a trip once, he had stepped off the train for some liquid refreshment. Returning to his compartment he was unable to locate a painting he had left there. He got hold of the conductor and declared solemnly:

"My name is Munch. I'm an Englishman of an old and famous family. While I was in the station restaurant getting a glass of beer someone stole a very costly picture. I lost it here on the train. You must find it—I *demand* that you find it immediately. If you don't have it back to me within an hour I shall have to report the matter to London. It might bring about war!"

The conductor soon found the picture exactly where Munch had left it. The painter had returned to the wrong compartment.

Among the many people Munch met in his Berlin period, August Strindberg was undoubtedly the most remarkable. Strange to say, they became friends of sorts although they were difficult individuals—stubborn and suspicious. Widely different in some respects, they shared a few peculiar ideas. Believing in strange powers and portents, they would scan a room carefully before entering—was it shaped like a coffin, or was it perhaps evil in some other way? However, their relationship never developed into a warm friendship. That they both fell in love with the same woman did not improve the situation.

"I painted a few pictures of these people," Munch said, "among them the one I have called *Jealousy*. It's that one with the green face in the foreground and a man who keeps looking at a nude woman. I had gone to Paris and was planning an exhibit there. Then these people came, and I had to pack up my pictures and move on. After all, I had painted *him* green and *her* in the nude. That Paris exhibit never came off. Had I been able to have a show there I might not have been reminded so often by critics that I received my name as a painter in Germany. To break through in Paris is a great thing for an artist in our days. That business with the woman in Berlin ruined a great deal for me."

While in Berlin, he painted August Strindberg, a portrait revealing an unmistakable awareness of the dramatist's greatness. Strindberg was unhappy with the painting, however, particularly because of the peculiar way in which Munch had painted in a frame. On one side of the picture the frame is marked by a few broken, straight lines which, on the opposite side, become softly arched and terminate in the figure of a woman. "My intention," Munch said, "was to frame Strindberg between the masculine and the feminine"—a notion that discloses a deeper knowledge of himself and the dramatist than he was aware of. In the lower left corner of the picture he had written "Stindberg" instead of "Strindberg". The entire matter infuriated Strindberg. He did not want any woman in the picture. And what did he mean calling him "Stindberg"? The next time he sat for Munch he brought a gun, put it on the table and stated in mock solemnity:

"I want no insinuations."

"Oh yes, Strindberg—I remember him well," said Munch much later. "He had hired a repulsive fellow named Paul—used him as valet and door mat. 'Get my coat,' he'd say, and Paul would run. Strindberg painted too—mood pictures of gray weather and storms. One evening he said to me: 'I'm the greatest painter in Scandinavia.'

"'If so,' I said, 'then I am Scandinavia's greatest poet. Skoal!'

"He just looked at me—perhaps he had been up too early, or he might have written all night long. Once I said, 'I hate everything and everybody, except myself.'

"'You're lucky,' Strindberg replied. 'I hate myself too.'"

In the Berlin period, Munch also met the Norwegian sculptor Gustav Vigeland and for a while shared an attic room with him.

"In our poverty we shared everything," Munch recalled, "even a girl friend. One evening I took her out, although it was really Vigeland's turn. When I came back and was on my way upstairs I saw Vigeland's burly figure at the top landing. As soon as I was in sight he ran back into the room and returned a moment later with a bust of me he had just finished. This he threw at me with great fury—barely missing. It frightened me so that I dashed out and ran all the way to the railway station and jumped onto a train. I surely didn't dare stay in Berlin as long as Vigeland was on the loose. He is mad as a hatter, Vigeland is. I don't think much of his art either. First he imitated Rodin, later Maillol, and then me. But that bust he threw at me was good—perhaps the best thing he ever did. Damned women!"

Munch and Vigeland never became friends again. To Munch it was a source of constant irritation to see Vigeland receive millions of *kroner* from the city of Oslo to complete his sculpture park while he, Munch, had to pay taxes. And Vigeland, who knew quite well that people suspected him of borrowing Munch's ideas, never hired a model who had sat for Munch. "Have you been with Munch? Aha. I see. Well, I can't use you."

In his earlier years, Munch met many people and had no objection to parties, but he was definitely no social lion. He made friends easily but rejected them as quickly, especially if they appeared nosy. For a party one time, he had prepared a speech. In getting dressed, he was unable to find his studs and hurriedly made some, which, at a distance, looked like red stones although they were actually match-heads fastened underneath with pins. Sitting tense and immobile during the dinner to keep the "stones" in place, he finally rose to deliver his speech and did not say a word. Having stood there in complete silence for a few moments, he sat down again.

"I knew the whole speech by heart," he said. "But suddenly I remembered that I had to say a few intro-ductory words before I started the speech itself. It was only after I had sat down again that it came to me—I should have said 'Ladies and gentlemen'."

Munch's Thoughts

Edvard Munch's life was a restless quest and a continuous anxiety. Unlike his father, he found no comfort in the Christian faith. Painting was his only comfort.

"For me, to paint is a disease and an intoxication," he said, "a disease I don't want to get rid of, an intoxication I crave. Now and then I read a little. I like to hear someone play, and I can sit in the theatre for a while too, but then I have to hurry home. This doesn't mean that I have to sit with the paint brush in my hand. I rarely do. Days, even weeks, may go by when I don't paint at all. But I keep struggling with my pictures even then. Mostly I go around waiting for the desire to paint. I can't stand to be far away from my charcoal sticks and my brushes. I must have the certainty that they are lying in readiness. In the morning, sometimes, I may find a picture I have painted during the night. In fact, many of my best pictures I have painted almost without knowing it. I'm an insomniac, and it's better to paint than to writhe in bed.

"I wanted to paint some apples. I have never really cared for still-lives, but I wanted very much to paint apples like Cézanne does it. Paint them in such way that I would want to eat them. I painted hundreds of apples —could not get the hang of it. It developed into a fixed idea. I simply had to find out whether I could paint one single apple. I must have kept it up for weeks, but it was no use. Then the message reached me that my grand-nephew—he who is named for me—had been stricken with tuberculosis. It was impossible to sit still—impossible to sleep. I took the train to Trondheim where he was hospitalized—a twelve hours trip. Went to the hospital but didn't have the strength to go in—just left a few parcels, then took the train back to Oslo. I arrived home late in the evening. And would you believe it? That night I sat before my canvas and painted a delicious apple."

Everything Edvard Munch painted reflects his own soul. Even when he had models the resulting pictures speak mostly of Munch. He did not care to paint "street faces"—faces which showed great likeness. Likeness was no criterion. It had to be a good picture.

Munch once wrote:

"I don't compete with the camera, and I have no fear of it as long as it cannot be used in heaven or hell. The habit of painting women knitting and men reading must come to an end. I'm going to paint human beings who breathe and feel, love and suffer. People must comprehend the sanctity of what I am trying to do and take off their hats, like in a church."

To Munch the sun was divine—the source of life and light. Solar bodies and the "powers" were living beings. The moon was a child of the earth, lava was petrified blood. With the moonlight came sexual drives and anxiety. Death was only a transformation. Man consisted of waves of spirit and matter. He could be dissolved and recreated into new forms. The eternal cycle continues. When a larva can become a butterfly, why couldn't man after death be transformed into something new—something we cannot see?

Man was an open receptacle in the process of being filled by the waves which flood towards it. All existence contributed to man: the woods, the flowers, the sea, and the air, even the stones on the shore lived and contributed to man's soul. Without all this, man himself was only a simple earthworm who loved and suffered—great only in his own thoughts. It is dangerous to dig too deeply into the crust of the earth—it might cause an earthquake. For him who was weary of dancing to the tune of destiny, there was only one way out—suicide.

From 1892 until his death, Munch attempted to paint his particular view of life. In the frieze he pictures life as a game of checkers with human beings as movable objects. Right or wrong, good or evil—what does this matter to the "powers"? Life has only one commandment: procreate—keep the blind game, life, going.

One of the paintings in *The Frieze of Life* Munch has titled *Toward the Light*. It shows a pillar of naked human beings who battle savagely to reach the top. Those already there are lifting a casket toward heaven.

Greater thinkers than Albert Kollmann, "the Faust I met in Berlin," have contributed to Munch's pessimistic view of life. His favorite writers were Ibsen, Dostoevski, Zola, and Strindberg, and among philosophers he found Kierkegaard, Schopenhauer, and Nietzsche challenging.

It was difficult for him to acquire knowledge of something that went contrary to his own opinions, while he found it easy to put stock in curious happenings. He believed in strange spirits and cultivated peculiar notions. He was convinced that the earth at one time had had two moons. This he had from Strindberg. One might find the second moon, he thought, by searching in the vicinity of the North Pole where it supposedly had fallen down.

He often revealed a lack of familiarity with the most matter-of-fact subjects. It is difficult to believe, but he actually recognized the moon only when it was full! He has drawn and painted the moon hundreds of times —but always round and full. One evening in 1936 we went for a walk and he said:

"What has happened to the moon? I was walking here just the other night in the brightest moonlight."

"There is the moon," I said and pointed to the half section in sight.

"That's not the moon," Munch said. "Don't you know that the moon is round?"

At times, it might seem as if the memory of something he had seen had become literally affixed to his optic nerve. To illustrate this he once related an episode:

"I stood looking at a white dog. Then a man came walking between me and the dog, the shadow of his leg casting a dark spot on the dog. Whether you believe it or not, I could see that dark spot on the dog long after the man had disappeared. I stood there staring at the dark spot and knew that it wasn't there. I have tried to paint a picture of it."

Munch was quick to flare up and slow to forget an insult. Finding it easy to believe that people wished him harm, he imagined he had enemies and secret opponents who were out to get him. A well-known Norwegian painter for whom he had no liking once sent him a poverty-stricken colleague. Arriving around nine in the evening, just as Munch had gone to bed, the visitor asked for a hand-out of ten *kroner*. Years thereafter Munch would say:

"I suffer from insomnia and prefer to go to bed early. Even so, I stay up until late in the night—waiting for the beggars my enemies send me.»

If he saw two people putting their heads together he would say:

"Look at them! What sort of devilish scheme are they brewing? Won't this bourgeois mob ever stop whispering about me?"

Women in particular aroused his suspicion.

"Regardless how you treat them they create problems," he said. "Worst of all are those you try most diligently to stay away from."

In 1908 he experienced a mental crisis rooted in this persecution complex. During this he might go so far as to strike people—even complete strangers—who sat whispering nearby, thinking they were saying something bad about him. To make matters worse, his physical condition had been rendered weak by excessive drinking.

"The only thing that would give me courage to cross the street back in 1908," he recalled, "was a good, strong drink—or even two or three."

He consulted a Dr. Christensen in Copenhagen but fled from his clinic after one night and instead checked in at the psychiatric establishment of Dr. Daniel Jacobsen in whose care he remained for almost eight months. During this interval he kept up his painting and even wrote a love poem, *Alpha and Omega,* which he illustrated.

His paintings from 1908 are neither more turbulent nor particularly different in other respects from those produced before his illness or after his recovery. Much later he explained it this way:

"Even during the periods of my greatest depression, a strange and soothing peace came over me when I painted —as if everything evil let go of me the moment I started."

The poem *Alpha and Omega*—illustrated by a series of lithographs somewhat less controlled technically than other works from the same period—reflects the mental and spiritual problems confronting him.

Even if a man travels to a deserted island with his woman, the poet states, he has no way of trusting her. Animals, even flowers, are his rivals, and the moon with its seductive power has male organs. He who desires to be true will be ripped apart, for all the forces of life are against him. Mankind consists of a mixture of the human and the animalistic.

Alpha, the man, and Omega, the woman, are the first human beings on the island. Asleep in the grass and enveloped in dreams, Alpha is playfully awakened by Omega. They enter the forest together. Though mysteriously dark, the forest abounds in bright, beautiful flowers and plants and strange animal life.

Caught by sudden fear, Omega throws herself passionately into Alphas arms, and for days thereafter the island vibrates in a flood of sunshine.

One day, when Alpha is farther back among the trees, Omega lies sunning herself at the edge of the forest. Suddenly a huge cloud spreads its cover across the sky and veils the island in its shadow. Alpha calls to Omega, but she does not respond. Emerging from the forest to search for her, he sees her sitting with the head of a serpent in her hands—a large serpent that has coiled itself around her lovely body and whose shiny eyes have

Alpha in their spell. Suddenly the cloud pours forth its rain, Omega again seeks Alpha, and the two flee together in fear.

Later, when Alpha encounters the serpent, he fights it and gives it the death blow while Omega watches from afar.

Omega meets the bear, and, feeling its soft fur against her body, puts her arms around its neck and sinks into the animal's furry softness.

Next she meets the poet—in the shape of a hyena whose fur is badly torn. Finding her usual phrases of love ineffective, Omega instead winds with her delicate hands a laurel wreath with which she crowns the hyena's unhappy head.

The tiger approaches, stretching its terrible, ferocious head toward Omega's enchantingly beautiful face. Unafraid, she places her tiny hand in the tiger's open jaw caressing the teeth of the wild beast.

Later, encountering the bear, the tiger senses Omega's fragrance—the odor of the pale apple blossoms which Omega showers with love and kisses every morning at sunrise. The beasts fight and tear each other asunder.

Now the position of the figures changes all of a sudden, as in a chess game, and Omega, rejecting the animals, clings to Alpha while the beasts of the forest, uncomprehending, stretch their necks and watch in wonderment.

Omega's eyes look different. Usually light blue, they become black with crimson spots when she gazes at her lover as she covers her mouth with a flower. But the interlude of harmony is brief. Again her desires turn toward the animals, and one day Alpha finds her on the shore kissing an ass whose head is resting in her lap. Heartbroken, he seeks out the ostrich and leans his head against its neck; but Omega does not see his grief, for she is totally absorbed in her favorite pastime—kissing.

Omega, saddened and weary by her inability to possess all the animals of the island, sits down in the grass and weeps bitterly, then runs in frenzied search throughout the island until she meets the swine. She falls on her

Portrett av Rolf Stenersen, 1925
Portrait of Rolf Stenersen, 1925
110 x 90 cm, Munch-museet, Oslo

Kunstnerens far, korpslege Christian Munch, i sofahjørnet, 1883
The Artist's Father, Doctor Christian Munch, in the Sofa, 1883
40 x 34 cm, Munch-museet, Oslo

Kunstnerens tante, Karen Bjølstad, i gyngestolen, 1883
The Artist's Aunt, Karen Bjølstad, in the Rocking Chair, 1883
47 x 41 cm, Munch-museet, Oslo

Det syke barn, 1896
The Sick Child, 1896
121,5 x 118,5 cm Konstmuseum, Göteborg

Sjalusi, 1895
Jealousy, 1895
67 x 100 cm, Rasmus Meyers samlinger, Bergen

Kunstnerens søster, Inger Munch, 1892
The Artist's Sister, Inger Munch, 1892
172 x 121 cm, Nasjonalgalleriet, Oslo

Kvinnen i tre stadier. Sfinx, 1894
The Tree Stages of Woman. The Sphinx, 1894
164 x 250 cm, Rasmus Meyers samlinger, Bergen

Livets dans, 1899
The Dance of Life, 1899
125,5 x 190,5 cm, Nasjonalgalleriet, Oslo

Pubertet, 1894-95
Puberty, 1894-95
151,5 x 110 cm, Nasjonalgalleriet, Oslo

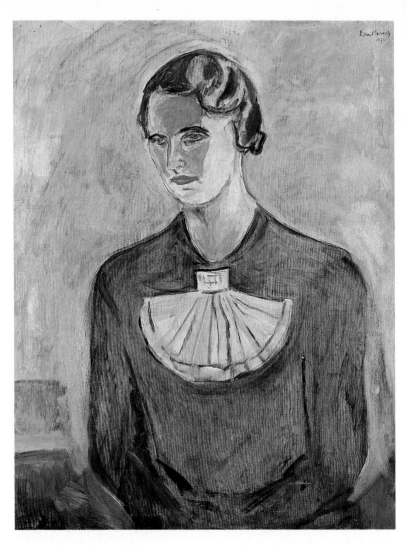

Portrett av Annie Stenersen, 1934
Portrait of Annie Stenersen, 1934
80 x 65 cm, privat eie. *Private collection.*

knees, her long black hair hiding her body, and she exchanges glances with the swine.

But her unhappiness persists. One night, when the golden pillar of the moon ripples in the water, Omega, carried on the back of a stag, flees out over the sea all the way to the irridescent green land under the moon—and Alpha is alone on the island.

In due time, Omega's children flock to him—a new generation of islanders calling him father—little swine, little serpents, little monkeys, other animals and human bastards. In utter despair Alpha runs along the shore, his hands pressing against his ears in an effort to shut out the shrieking sound in the air. Sky and sea are covered with blood, earth and sky and sea tremble—all is total anguish.

The stag returns with Omega on its back.

Alpha sits by the shore and allows her to approach. Sensing the blood rushing in his ears, feeling his muscles swell, he lays hand on the unfaithful and beats her to death. Then bending over her dead body, he is struck by her singular expression—the very same expression her face had revealed that moment in the forest long ago when he had loved her the most—and sinks into deep contemplation of her beauty and the memory of their brief happiness. In this state, he is attacked by all her children —the animals of the island—and torn to pieces. A new generation fills the island.

Already prior to his stay with Dr. Jacobsen, Munch had altered his color preferences and begun to paint more brightly. After his release, his colors became even more intence. Yet, it is in the choice of subjects that the greatest change is to be found. These are no longer predominantly melancholy and dark; and the purely pictorial elements —the rise and fall of lines, the division of surfaces, the color interplay—take on greater importance than the latent emotional impact of the subject matter.

The months in Dr. Jacobsen's care did not purge him of his inhibitions and pecularities. After all, it was no spiritual cure he had gone through. It was, nevertheless, in a small measure, a miraculous cure, for he left the hospital healthier than ever, quite able to take care of himself.

From 1910 to 1920, he abstained completely from alcohol. Thereafter, it happened that he went on a spree. However, as soon as he noticed that drinking weakened his ability to work, he became an abstainer again.

"In fact, all I drink now is a glass of champagne before I go to the dentist," he said. "Often I let him wait. I can't stand the thought of having him drill away that gentle intoxication."

In his later years, Munch refrained from eating meat. He rarely smoked, drank tea instead of coffee, and stayed away from all sorts of pills and medicine.

"Jacobsen was a fine physician," he said, reminiscing about his stay in the hospital. "He walked around like a pope among white nurses and pale patients. The food was white too—everything was white except Jacobsen. *I* wanted to say something too, so I asked him to pose for me. I placed him in the picture, big and strutting in a fire of color like all hell. Then he pleaded with me—became tame like a pigeon.

"'Let's have a drink, Jacobsen,' I said.

"'You really want to?' he asked.

"'No,' I said. 'It's only that *I* want to be able to say something too. What color should I give your beard? Aren't you a little knock-kneed, Jacobsen? I do wonder who is going to buy this picture.'

"Jacobsen, the pope, wanting to be neither knock-kneed nor greenbearded, become my prisoner.

"Don't you believe for a minute that it is easy to get out of such a clinic! If anyone should get me committed to a place like that now, I'm not sure I would have the strength to recover. When they ask you something you don't answer the way you'd *like* to; instead, you have to consider the question carefully and try to decide what they *want* you to say. If you can't come up with the exact answers you'll never get out."

Twenty years after Munch had been released from the clinic, he met Dr. Jacobsen in the street but failed to recognize him.

"Don't you remember me?" Jacobsen asked.

Munch looked at him.

"What in blazes ... if it isn't Dr. Jacobsen! But you have changed color completely!"

Ludvig Karsten, noted Norwegian painter and contemporary of Munch, was notorious for his riotous living. His relationship to Munch was much like that of a disciple to the master, and Munch, who rarely expressed his opinion of a fellow artist, often spoke favorably about Karsten, although he may have been irritated by his disciple's tendency to utilize subject matters identical to his own. Karsten's treatment of these, however, differs sharply from Munch's. Karsten is no mystic. He paints boldly and rapidly with energetic brush strokes in a highly individualistic style, in tune with—but hardly imitative of—Edvard Munch.

"Of course, you must realize that Karsten was no evil man," Munch said shortly after Karsten's death. "An evil man can't paint like that. In my opinion, Karsten developed his devilish schemes simply to conceal that he was both weak and kind. You have heard about the time he bought four bottles of brandy and handed them in through the window in an old folks home, haven't you? It was a hell of a mess. One of the old fellows tumbled down the stairs—broke his neck and died.

"'The man was drunk,' Karsten explained to me. 'He didn't feel a thing.'

"Perhaps that's why Karsten drank so much—was too sensitive to be sober. It isn't easy to be a human being, you know. Everyone can't be sly as a snake, tame as a pigeon, and ferocious as a tiger. Yet that's what it takes to find your way in the world.

"Once, after a heavy drinking bout, Karsten and I had a fist fight. Having thrown him down the stairs—he wasn't much of a fighter, you see—I brought out my rifle, aimed at him, and fired. What if I hadn't missed?" He shuddered at the thought. "I have tried to paint that scene," he continued, "but all I could make of it was a landscape in the summer night and a man taking aim with a rifle."

To Edvard Munch painting was the fulfillment of life's demand. To be an artist constantly striving to reach the ultimate of his own potential was to approach perfection and become reconciled with life itself.

Rabindranath Tagore, Indian poet and Nobel laureate, came to Oslo and delivered a lecture on art in which he claimed that the spiritual contents of art played a greater role in the Orient than it did in the West. The lecture was delivered in the *Aula*, the University Festivital Hall, where the distinguished visitor was confronted with Edvard Munch's monumental murals. Munch's art appealed to him instantly, and before he left Oslo he had occasion to purchase one of his paintings. A few years later a close friend of Tagore's visited Oslo and brought greetings to Munch. It was my privilege to bring him to the artist's home and act as interpreter.

Tagore's friend bowed deeply to Munch and said:

"My lord and friend, Rabindranath Tagore, has asked me to extend to you his most humble greetings. He treasures your painting as the pearl of his collection."

Munch asked me to return the greeting and express his gratitude, then to inquire of the Indian visitor what he thought about life after death.

The Indian felt we would have to live our lives over again, until we became pure and virtuous.

Munch then asked if the Indian knew anyone so pure and virtuous that he might not have to live his life over.

"Few are perfect," the visitor replied. "I know only one, Mahatma Gandhi."

"What about Tagore?" Munch wondered. "Might not he be another?"

"My lord is a great master," Tagore's friend said,

"perhaps India's greatest living poet. But he must live his life over again."

"If an artist is to reach the highest potential in his art he will simply have no time to visit the sick and care for the poor," Munch said highly irritated. "Tell him that and ask if Tagore has not dedicated himself totally to his art and if he has not reached his own highest potential by being an artist."

The Indian repeated: "My lord, Tagore, is a great master. But he must, like the rest of us, live his life over again."

Munch stared at him—speechless. Then he took a step forward and bowed so deeply that he lost his balance and nearly fell over. By a few rapid steps he regained control, however, and, passing me on his way through the room, said in exasperation: "Get him out of here—damn it!"

At the Canvas

For weeks Edvard Munch might struggle mentally with a subject before committing it to the canvas. Often, new inspirations would come while he painted; in the main, however, he knew what the picture would be like before he painted a single stroke. Even with his model before him he painted from memory. If he did cast an eye on the model it was mostly to refresh his memory on minor points in the picture he had ready in his mind. For this reason, it was easy to model for Munch. There was no need to sit still; if the model wanted to stir it was quite all right. Often he painted without moving his eyes from the canvas.

"I do prefer to have the model—or the landscape itself—before me," he explained. "It makes me feel freer. After all, I might have forgotten something."

So preoccupied with his painting might he become that he would not even notice it if his model got up and left. When he was to paint my two boys—then six and ten years old—he arrived by taxi and insisted on staying right in the car during the sketching. Eventually, however, he moved into the garden to continue his work there, keeping up a continuous monologue while he put up his canvas, arranged paints and brushes, and laid out the picture. After a while, the youngest of the boys—finding it impossible to stand still—stepped out of his position and left, and shortly thereafter the other followed suit. Munch painted and chatted and never took his eyes off the canvas:

"You're good boys to stand there as nicely as you do. Now, take the children I painted the other day, they didn't stand quietly for a single moment—they even began to throw stones. But you're standing there so nicely. Well, look at that—that was a lucky stroke. I feel sure this is going to be good. You certainly are nice boys. Now, the other ones—I wanted two thousand *kroner* for the picture. 'Two thousand *kroner!*' said the father, 'for two hours?' 'Twenty years and two hours,' I replied. He took me to court on it ... Now we'll add a little red here. My word, you're good boys. Look at that one—he's like a nobleman, isn't he? The other one looks like a face at the farmer's market."

He finished the picture—it did not matter that the boys had run out on him.

My wife and I met Munch in the theatre one evening.

"Why don't you come out to me some day soon. I'd like to paint you in all your finery. Call me up in a few days, won't you?»

When I called he said: "I don't remember what it was I wanted to paint. Perhaps some other time."

If he painted portraits it happened that he measured his models by squinting them, holding up a brush handle —but not often. Usually, he started out by sketching the main outline of the picture with charcoal. If the result was satisfactory he would often bring out a clean canvas and copy exactly what he had drawn before; then he would add a few colors. As soon as he approved of the result he would bring out a third canvas to which he would transfer the second sketch, altering details as he went along. Working stepwise in this manner, he would not lose sight of his original plan for the picture in progress.

In all his portraits, Munch wanted to express his own opinion of the individual portrayed—probe more deeply than a photograph would do.

"I can't paint people I don't know," he said.

In doing a portrait of my wife, he painted her eyes blue.

"I know her eyes are green," he reasoned, "but their *effect* is blue. She is not the type to have green eyes. As a rule, those with green eyes have red hair, long pointed noses, and thin lips. Your wife is quiet and good—is unaware of the true nature of her sex. So her eyes had to be painted blue. The effect of a color spot changes with the colors around it. I have painted her at the moment she wants to ask you something but is uncertain whether she ought to."

My wife, because she preferred to be painted facing the artist, saw to it that she always turned directly toward him. Munch never asked her to change position. Even so, in the finished painting she is facing half to the side. Usually, he painted portraits full face.

"The side view tends to show racial and ancestral features," he commented. "The full face tells more of the person himself."

Every year, as if determined to record the result of the passing of time, he produced a self-portrait. Appearing tired and morose in most of these—there is never a trace of a smile—he is always portrayed older and more decrepit than he really is—an attempt, perhaps, to soften the psychological effect of the advent of old age. A few years before his death, he portrayed himself fully prepared to meet his end.

Munch painted a vision as *he* saw it—one single visual image. He does not portray objects as a person would see them by moving his eyes. Everything in the direct line of vision is distinct and sharp; peripheral matters, on the other hand, are always vague and sketchy.

An untiring experimenter, he tried everything—sometimes even squirting colors onto the canvas. Had he labored long and fruitlessly he might threaten his picture:

"Watch out or I'll give you a shower!"

Or he might subject the picture to a more fiendish penalty by leaving it out in the open at the mercy of the sun and rain for weeks—a treatment he called the "horse cure." As a result, he might by accident discover new color effects that would give him the necessary impetus to continue working on the canvas.

"My pictures seem to need a bit of sunshine, some dirt, and a little rain to bring about the color harmony," he commented. "There is something harsh about them when they are completely fresh. For that reason, it worries me when people clean and polish them. A little dirt and a few holes in the canvas help the pictures along, I think. Only those who keep painting brown and yellow and black have reason to be afraid of a little dirt—perhaps because they have added so much of it themselves."

In the technical progress of his painting Munch revealed the amazing assurance of a sleepwalker. The varying weight elements of the picture surfaces create a meaningful balance, and centers of gravity are always arranged in such a way that the pictures quite naturally seem to hang straight. Colors which appear to "run" gravitate according to natural laws.

He loved spatial effects, and his pictures always extend into great depth. Placing a distinct object in the foreground, he would sink his eyes far into the background —thousands and thousands of feet.

There are other easily identifiable features. After the shooting accident in which he lost part of his right middle finger, he rarely painted hands.

"Fingers are naked and repulsive," he shuddered. "I can't stand people who fidget around with their hands."

So hands are usually hidden or, when shown, appear rigid and chiseled. Fingernails he never painted. Only in the self-portrait with a cigarette from the 1890's has he paid particular attention to the hands. They are, however, not his own—a friend posed for that part of the portrait.

He was equally reluctant in the painting of a woman's breasts and almost always sketched this body feature very casually. The same with ears—they are never distinct.

Munch, who painted death scenes and repulsive visions of agony, hesitated painting those parts of the body which he did not like. In this respect, he had something in common with Edgar Allan Poe—pathologically preoccupied with anguish and horror yet chaste in spirit.

On his palette were all sorts of colors except black. Instead of black, he used a shade of dark-blue that tends to give the impression of black. Although his technical approach changed constantly, most of his pictures are readily recognized as his and only his. Lines and shapes emerge in accordance with mysterious subconscious rules. His lines—undulating, long, and never sharp—float freely like a river in a landscape. On the edges, objects are merely suggested. Certain arcs recur with haunting regularity. Foliage is invariably painted as a collective mass. The moon, we recall, is always full, usually reflected in the fjord, an irridescent pillar underneath. A similar technique is applied in act paintings when he pictures the male organ. So afraid of repeating the same form from painting to painting, he still could not resist developing one fixed symbol—the phallic. It is as common in his works as his signature.

His tendency to split figures into several groups intensifies the mood of his composition.

"I don't like anything that comes in threes," he said. "Three people together have something ominous about them. Only two can converse; all the third person can do is interrupt, enter into the conversation either to show off or to befriend the one and reject the other."

In a keen awareness of the danger of artistic regidity and personal mannerism, Edvard Munch searched tirelessly for new expressive means. Few have struggled as hard as he did in this respect. He was always trying to avoid repeating color combinations and brush strokes he had used before and he rarely worked of canvases of the same height and width as those he had recently completed. His paintings were narrow or wide, tall or short, although his preference seemed to be large canvases and broad brushes. Curiously enough, when he returned to subjects he had treated before—which he did quite often—he insisted on using canvases of the exact size and shape as those used for the same subject previously. In such cases, however, he was particularly careful not to repeat brush strokes and color combinations. Many of his best-known subjects were painted time and again, but no two paintings, even when viewed superficially, give the same impression.

Subconscious ideas are frequent in his pictures—strange spots and curious lines, especially along the edges. Asked why this or that had been included, he might answer: "I felt that particular area needed something."

Although he liked to talk while he painted he was no conversationalist. If a comment would interrupt his line of thought he would put his brush down, annoyed, and blurt out: "Don't you see I'm painting!"

He would wipe his brushes on his clothes and then complain about the spots. "Please see to it that I don't spot this new suit," he told me once when he was in the process of painting.

"Why not put on an old coat?"

"That's a splendid idea."

He removed the new one and disappeared into the bedroom to find another only to return without a coat. He continued to paint but stopped suddenly and said:

"Isn't it a bit cold here? I've got to put on my coat." He picked up the one he had just taken off.

"But that's the new one."

"What the devil ... so it is!" Surprised, he went into the bedroom again but showed up once more in his shirt sleeves and resumed his painting.

"No, it's too cold in here. I'm freezing."

He put down his brush, went back into the bedroom, returned, and put on the new coat he had removed earlier.

"Didn't you want to put on an old coat?"

He looked at me, visibly irritated, and said: "What's the meaning of this? Don't you see I'm working?"

When in later years Munch smoked a cigar it was mostly to keep his guests company, and he would soon put the cigar down. This happend once when he was painting a portrait of a Norwegian banker who was well known for his stinginess and for his constant worry that

Norway's import would exceed her export so that her gold resources would dwindle.

"I don't like that man," Munch said. "Every time he is out here and I've gotten a good start on my work he interrupts me and says: 'Are you only smoking half of your cigar?'

"Does it make sense that I bother to answer such trivial questions while I'm trying my best to make a good picture?

"'Whom do you prefer to look like,' I ask. 'Goethe or Gandhi?'

"He is a strong man and doesn't take his eyes off mine for a moment. First I wanted to portray him as a pirate, but I soon realized that would be wrong and instead painted him as an exhausted mountain climber."

Once, when he had already put on his hat and coat to go out for a walk, he suddenly became aware of the badly torn wallpaper in his bedroom. He looked at it for a while, then, still with hat and coat on, stepped up onto the bed and started to paint.

"Why don't you sit down and wait for a minute," he asked. "I got such a sudden urge to paint. It's going to be spirits—good spirits guarding my bed. You know, I've never painted spirits before. Of course, there are spirits—there's so much we human beings can't see or understand. Now, spiritualism, that's something else. When that man recently testified in court that the spirit had been tugging his arms he was merely revealing that he suffered from rheumatism."

The walk had to be postponed to another day. When he had finished painting he was too tired to go out. We moved his bed into another room, and he went to sleep.

Those who modeled in Oslo all wanted to pose for Edvard Munch. He paid well and was courteous and kind. He liked to chat with his models, and often, when he was too tired to paint, he would invite them into his living room and serve tea and cookies—wine, too, sometimes. They were paid by the hour, even when he did not paint.

It happened that young girls would try to develop a more intimate relationship with him. This put him on his guard. One evening, a beautiful girl fainted while modeling. When she came to again on the floor Munch treated her with great tenderness—bathed her temples with cold water, offered her some brandy, and wrapped her in his best blanket. In response to her smile and expression of gratitude, however, he brushed her aside:

"Imagine the hell the newspapers would have given me if you had died right here in my house! I really don't dare use you anymore—please, don't come back."

When Munch wanted to emphasize a point he'd often take a pencil and start drawing. "This is what I have in mind," he would say and hold up the drawing.

He might become so entranced by a sight that he would remain in a spot even when actual danger threatened. This happened in Berlin in the 1930's when he witnessed a murder in the street. A bomb, thrown at a passing car, exploded with devasting effect and people scurried for shelter. Only Munch remained. When a degree of normalcy was restored and people came out of hiding Munch rushed to his hotel and asked the clerk for a sheet of paper. Sitting in the lobby, he began to sketch what he had seen.

"This is the way it was," he said, showing the drawing to other guests. "The explosion carried the man in the car high up in the air. Do you think he was killed?"

A summer day, when a fire raged near Munch's home, he came running with his canvas and paint box and took up position so close to the spot that the firemen had to ask him to move.

"Can't you see I'm working?" Munch complained. "And couldn't you possibly wait a minute or two with that hose over there? You don't want me to paint only smoke, do you?"

The Landscape

Edvard Munch was deeply attached to his own landscape and did not care to stay away for any length of time. To him, Oslo and its fjord were home—everywhere else he felt alien and restless. Although he has painted scenes from Germany and France, the soft contours of the Oslofjord region are the leitmotif of his landscape art.

Born in Løten, a rural community eighty miles north of Oslo, he moved with his family to the capital shortly after his mother's death, and his childhood memories all center around Oslo.

He wanted to live—as most Norwegians do—in a place overlooking the sea. He did not travel much in his own country and had no desire to see the community in which he was born, the south coast, the Fjord Country of the West, North Norway, or the inland valleys and mountain plateaus. Yet he traveled abroad a great deal, but only to see art. He visited Sweden, Denmark, France, Switzerland, and Italy—and time and again Germany. In France, it was *what* he saw that inspired him; in Germany, where he had friends of long-standings, it was *whom* he saw.

Almost all his trips abroad took place in the so-called dark months. In the summer, he preferred to stay home. In fact, he did not mind staying home in the winter either as long as the fields were white with snow. It was the darkness that depressed him. His winter landscapes, often nocturnal, glow with an intense light of cold, snow, and ice.

It was no accident that the first property Munch purchased was located in Aasgaardstrand, a village some seventy miles south of the capital, for he had been attracted to this Oslofjord hamlet ever since his first days as a painter.

The house, facing a village street, had three small rooms. In the back was a little garden which Munch neglected. He cared neither for flowers nor fruit and let the garden grow wild.

He did nothing to make his house pleasant and home-like either; disliking any other form of physical labor than that involved in painting, he just kept everything the way it was. The furniture was not only simple and proletarian, it was downright ugly. There was two beds, a table, and a few straight chairs. Everywhere the dust lay thick and the mess was incredible. In the wood box might be a paper bag with hard rusks, on the dining table brushes, rusty nails, paste, and other sticky items. This was the house in which Munch felt at home and which he loved more than any other place on earth.

It must have been the shoreline of the village and the humble houses along the narrow, steep streets that had such a relaxing effect on him. Here he found *his* land-scape—the countryside, the lines, and the relationships which best suited his temperament. He could watch the soothing sight of the sun rising above the fjord while the low but steep hills to the west obstructed his view of the sunset. "It chills me to see the sun go down," he said. "Everything suddenly becomes so still. I don't like to see anything die."

And he thought the village so uniquely cozy—so comforting in his loneliness. The course of every street was familiar to him, the feature of each house; he knew what people did and who they were. So little was veiled in secrecy—no villager was a stranger. With his perceptive eyes he could see and follow everything.

When he bought the little place he was a poor and controversial figure. To the people of Aasgaardstrand, however, he was still "the artist from the capital."

Edvard Munch has painted just about every possible subject in the little town—the houses, the streets, the bridge leading to the steamer landing, and the beach—

always the beach. Strange to say, he painted few pictures of the people, and when he did paint them, as in *Girls on the Bridge,* he never revealed individual features. They were just young girls standing anonymously on a bridge.

When he painted the beach he liked to have someone sitting on the boulders near the shore, but his model was almost always his sister, Inger, or it might be his friend from Oslo, Jappe Nielsen. Even in Aasgaardstrand, he stayed away from people. It was the landscape—the streets, the houses, the shore—that elevated and inspired him, not the people.

Munch's feeling for a landscape was extraordinarily sensitive, not only in regard to his painting. A landscape might oppress him, or he might find it confusing or ominous. Having a marked fear of open places, he found it in his youth difficult to cross a street and, strange as it may sound, he did not like to look around. Perhaps that is why Munch, living most of his life in mountainous Norway, never painted a mountain landscape—nothing steeper than the low hills west of Aasgaardstrand. The mere sight of a mountain was enough to make him dizzy. This dizziness and his fear of open places he has pictured in paintings and graphic works—most notably in *The Cry,* a subject also alluded to in the closing portion of his poem *Alpha and Omega. The Cry* shows a young person on a bridge, both hands clutching his head and the mouth open as if to reduce the impact of the sound. The sky is blood-red and the lines of the landscape tower around and above him in wildly winding arches. Under the lithograph of this subject, Munch wrote—in German—"I felt the cry of Nature." Rarely resorting to written texts, he must have been particularly anxious to have the public comprehend this work.

The Cry, perhaps Munch's most deeply personal picture, pours forth a terrifying agony as the artist tries to show how a landscape's colors and lines may represent a threat to an unbalanced, hypersensitive individual who suddenly one evening feels totally paralyzed by the landscape as lines and colors close in on him with suffocating reality.

His mouth twists into a cry of agony, and yet he is unable to utter a sound. This was Munch's own experience. He had realized then that something was wrong, that his nerves were on edge, but had been reluctant to seek a doctor's help, for he had thought his illness—his edgy nerves—contributed to his art. He did not want to be an average citizen, to lose his special characteristics. He wanted to be the painter Edvard Munch.

"What I have to give are these pictures of mine—without them I am nothing."

When Munch went for a walk he remained totally closed to the surroundings, so engrossed in his own thoughts that he seemed like a sleepwalker. If he opened his eyes widely the effect of what he saw was novel and strong—as if he suddenly saw things especially clearly. This is why he drifted into the habit of painting from memory—to reap the harvest of such an instantaneous vision.

"I don't paint what I see but what I saw."

He liked to stand out in the open and paint, but his eyes were fixed on the canvas all the time. Thus, he closed himself in even when he was outside. In his later years, he built himself open studios, twelve feet high and sixty feet long. Standing in these studios, he saw only the canvases and the gray walls—had to look up to get a glimpse of the sky. Most of those who do not love landscapes love the stars. They have a yearning only the starry sky can satisfy. The stars are a bridge of light suspended above them. Munch said that nature was far from dark when the stars were ablaze. He painted the evening sky often, but not as spots of light. Rather, he let the entire firmament shimmer.

A factual, faithful rendition of a landscape was of no interest to him. In his pictures, lines and colors were dictated by suddenly emerging ideas. He moved trees about and changed colors and forms to suit his own imagination. Here, too, likeness was no criterion—it had to be a good picture. Consequently, it is difficult to find the exact trees or house or place he painted. If we disregard paintings from his early youth, we find that those from Aasgaardstrand are just about the only ones that can be clearly identified by place. This shows that the Aasgaardstrand landscape was "homey" to him. Other scenes he approached with greater resistance; they had to be corrected to become "good pictures."

When Munch finally decided to move away from Asgaardstrand he did so because he was afraid his art might become stale by constant exposure to the same landscape. He needed new impressions—and in 1908 rented a property in Kragerø, a coastal town about a hundred miles south of Aasgaardstrand. There he found the scenic outlines that provided inspiration for two of the giant murals painted for the *Aula* of Oslo University —*The History* and *The Sun*.

The History presents a desolate landscape near the sea. The barren soil has brought forth a single gnarled, mighty oak tree whose powerful roots seem to draw nourishment from the rocky ground itself. At the base of the tree an aged man sits telling stories to a little boy. This entire canvas in its simplicity is a grandiose picture of Norway —barren and naked with rocks and sea. Like the oak tree, the Norwegian people have drawn nourishment from stones and water, defied the cold, conquered want. Now the old man shows the boy the land, tells him how it all came about. This is Norway—harsh and cold, but it is yours and mine. Here, where your roots are you will thrive, grow big and strong like the oak tree.

The Sun, principal mural in the Aula decorations, recalls the painter's vision of an early summer morning. In contrast, some of his finest winter scenes were also painted in Kragerø. Despite the fresh inspiration provided by the new landscape, however, Munch did not really come to terms with it. He was, in the Norwegian sense of the word, an Easterner, and Kragerø, on the border between East and South, presented a landscape too barren for him; even the woods on this threshold to the South were less dense than in the East. A few years later, he leased a property at Jeløya, a fertile island in his beloved Oslofjord, and during his stay there fields and meadows formed his principal subjects as shown in paintings such as *People Plowing, The Grain Harvest, Man in the Cabbage Field,* and *Path between White Birches.* Still, even Jeløya was not *his* landscape. He found it too fertile. "I can't live long among fields and meadows, cows and pigs," he said. So in 1911 he purchased a fair-sized property farther up the fjord where the soil was not quite as rich. This was Ramme in Hvitsten where he could look across the fjord toward Aasgaardstrand, the only place on earth where he had ever felt at home.

Mother Earth and a few of the smaller side decorations in the Aula project were painted in Hvitsten. But the place did not satisfy him. Feeling a strong urge to get across the fjord, he bought himself a boat. However, he had a tendency to get seasick, so the boat was mostly idle.

In 1916 he acquired his largest property, Ekely in the outskirts of Oslo. Munch rarely took advantage of the unobstructed view of the fjord which Ekely afforded. As cats save their sharp claws for battle, he used his eyes prudently in order to see more deeply when it counted.

Ekely—the Shelter of the Oaks—is a valuable property. The main building has eight rooms, and there are also barn, greenhouse, a large garden, and almost ten acres of tilled land. There were cows and horses as well. Munch, decidedly not interested in farming or gardening, sold the cows, neglected the garden—and painted the horses.

It is difficult to determine whether Munch liked it at Ekely or not. He had bought the place primarily to find room for *The Frieze of Life*—wanted to see the entire series hung in one place. This he never did at Ekely. After all, as time passed he decided to include in the frieze practically all the paintings he was satisfied with, and this made it a physical impossibility to hang more than a small portion of the frieze at one time. Most of the canvases stood around in his open-air studios, although many were hanging on or leaning against the walls of the many rooms in his house.

He often regretted having purchased Ekely—didn't care for his immediate neighbors. They all belonged to the Oslo "mob", a collective term he had devised to describe all those he did not like who lived in and around the capital.

Most of the landscapes painted at Ekely are readily identified. Very often he painted the barn, but never without changing form and color from painting to painting. The main building and the view toward the fjord he never painted.

He was fond of the city of Oslo itself. "The location is so wonderful," he said. "Oslo could have been one of the most beautiful cities in the world; the air—so mild and clear. But to walk down Karl Johan Street might cost me a thousand *kroner*," he lamented.. "Practically everyone I know needs money. 'Good morning, Edvard,' they say. 'How nice to meet you. I surely don't see you very often. Do you remember the days when you had no more than a couple of *kroner* in your pocket and didn't dare use them?' Well, he gets a thousand *kroner,* and I grab a taxi and go home."

Despite the unbearable "mob" Munch did feel at home in Oslo. When I asked what he had decided to do with his collection, he said: "Oslo will get it. It's best for the pictures—they belong here. Actually, I ought to give some of them to Germany where my name first became known. But in these days, when airplanes can whisk a person from country to country in a wink, artists ought to keep their pictures in their homelands. Besides, everything is so topsy-turvy in Germany after Hitler came to power.

"When you come to think of it, though, it's terrible that Oslo is to get my pictures ... the press was awful to me, especially *Aftenposten*. Even after Editor Schibsted's death, it was bad. *Aftenposten* practically starved me to death. Even so, they sent a journalist out here on my seventieth birthday. By that time I was so well known that it was no longer necessary to slaughter me.

"'Are you from *Aftenposten?*' I asked. 'Well then, get the hell out of here!'"

Aasgaardstrand was the only place he truly longed for. Wherever he went he brought the Aasgaardstrand contours with him. Even the landscapes he painted in Germany and France reveal these familiar features, and so does the series of theatre paintings he was commissioned to do for Max Reinhardt. Perhaps the desire to paint scenery came to him only when the subject in one way or another reminded him of "his" landscape, the fruit of a lengthy search—the stony shore of Aasgaardstrand where the sea and the sky embrace the earth, where the light plays a uniquely mystic role; where men and women in strife and tension stand rooted to the ground, completely at home in the landscape—merging with it—immobile like trees on a still summer day, or gently swaying like branches in the soft breeze of the summer night.

"Have you ever walked along that shore and listened to the sea?" he reminisced. "Have you ever noticed how the evening light dissolves itself into night? I know no place that has such a beautiful lingering twilight—isn't it sad that I have painted everything that there is to paint down there? To walk about in the village is like walking among my own pictures. I always get such a strong urge to paint when I go for a walk in Aaasgaardstrand."

Woman and Death

Doctor Munch loved his five children, but as a lonely, strict, and brooding Pietist he created a depressing and confined atmosphere in the home. His ceaseless Bible reading and devotional contemplation put a damper on the children's playfulness. They had little opportunity to be with others.

Tenderness toward the children was never sexually released, not even in the most modest sense of the word, for the woman of the house was not present as mother, or even as woman, only as aunt and housekeeper.

Of his mother, Edvard must have had only the vaguest recollection. In his many works based on childhood memories, she is present only twice, once in a drawing entitled *The Journey* in which she stands by a window dressed in traveling clothes, two children holding on to the hem of her skirt; and then in a painting called *The Odor of Death,* never exhibited.

Pietism, sickness, and death haunted his childhood like a never-ending nightmare and became an obsession from which he tried in vain to free himself through his art.

In the large canvas entitled *Melancholy,* he recalls a visit to his sister Laura. It was a bright sunny day when he called on her in the asylum and found her enveloped in an impenetrable darkness, withdrawn into her own world. She failed to recognize him, remained mute and immobile. In the painting, the golden daylight, streaming in through the large windows, is catching a bouquet of bright flowers placed on a fiery red table cloth. It is the contrast he has wanted to portray, the sunlight and the strong fresh colors without and the dark, hopeless night within.

Equally melancholy are the pictures of his brother and of his sister Inger. His brother, whom he always spoke of with great warmth, has been pictured while reading a book. Inger, the only one in the family who survived him, appears frequently in his paintings, and whatever he possessed of tenderness he showered upon these pictures—each brush stroke a somber caress.

He also produced a number of pictures of his father. The one to which he alluded when recalling the argument regarding the duration of the agony in hell was made into a woodcut which shows the father kneeling in prayer. In all other pictures we see him reading—the mood always dark and tragic. Children tend to feel, more keenly than adults, the oppressive sadness of silence. The nature of a person's faith often reflects his childhood experiences. Edvard Munch did not believe in divine grace, nor in an almighty and all-knowing Creator. Rather, he believed the Creator kept to himself, struggling with greater matters than human beings and their daily welfare.

"I don't know anyone who could read fairytales and sagas the way father did," Munch recalled. "He liked to talk about ghosts too and scared us every once in a while. He should never have become a physician—a poet would have been more like it.

"After mother died he became so old. The Bible is a thick book with fine print. No one who reads the Bible finishes the book. Father's intentions were so good, still he was stubborn and strict—a sincere and loveable person whom I looked up to and was afraid of, but whom I often felt sorry for. Haunted by thousands of fears, often afraid in his professional concern that he had not cleaned everything sufficiently, he tried so hard to do everything right. I do remember thinking him very impractical—not particularly good in his field, I thought. I wanted to give him a hand, but that didn't work. No one could talk to him."

In losing his mother, Edvard Munch in a way lost his

father too. They never became close friends who could talk together about all sorts of things. Soon after, he suffered another loss. His young aunt, whom he loved so deeply, drifted away from him. This he never quite got over.

These experiences—his many losses as a child—are at the root of his pessimism, his shyness, his loneliness and anxiety. Considering their childhood circumstances, it is not strange that only one of Doctor Munch's children ventured into marriage—Edvard's younger brother whose marital plans he opposed. Six months after the wedding, the young man died.

"He should not have gone through with it," Munch reasoned. "From father's side of the family we inherited poor nerves. Grandfather became mad, you know. Then there was mother's lung weakness. Of course, there was nothing wrong with my young sister-in-law, but she was too exuberant—insisted on the marriage. He was too weak for it—that's why he died so soon."

Man's drive may force him, subconsciously, into an attempt to re-establish the type of environment that characterized his childhood. Most people find the greatest measure of comfort and security under circumstances that seem familiar. Everything new and unexpected evokes fear—the new requires a long period of adjustment.

As Doctor Munch preferred loneliness, so Edvard seemed unable to live close to others. Too often he had experienced the loss of a loved one; therefore, to protect himself against new losses, he became withdrawn and suspicious, deathly afraid to show tenderness. He considered it a threat and a persecution if anyone tried to approach him.

"When my enemies feel confident they have me surrounded," he declared proudly, "I carry out one bold sortie—like Napoleon. Under the cover of darkness I break out of my beleaguered fortress and make my way through enemy lines, find a train, and leave. Then chaos reigns in the enemy camp. Frightened they run back and forth repeating, 'Where is he now? Where is he now?'"

His craving for tenderness and friendship evokes a sweet dream: people pursue him to make friends. But the dream changes—friends become enemies and persecution follows.

A healthy person's sexual drive demands a companion to share his desire. The sex drive is also a social drive. By this token, the recluse does not necessarily have reduced sexual desires; it is his *social* drive—his ability to join a fellow human being—that is paralyzed. Headstrong and self-centered, the recluse believes in his own superiority. Setting himself the loftiest goal, he is willing to sacrifice his own physical joys—and the joys of those near him—on the altar of this goal. The very striving toward its attainment is more important than the enjoyment of life itself. Brain and willpower alone count; bodily functions are a plague—he forgets that man is also an animal.

Such a recluse was Munch. Fleeing from life and from people, he withdrew into his work—his art—and failed to find the mental and physical equilibrium necessary to reap happiness from life itself, from the simple, everyday functions—breathing and moving about, choosing and rejecting, getting something started, the joy of working with others, of loving and being loved.

Edvard Munch felt very close to his family. It made him worried and restless to learn that a relative was sick. "There's nothing but sickness and death in our family," he would say; "it's in our blood."

Eager to help on such occasions, he would send money, but could never make himself spend time with his family. Even his sister Inger, the subject of so many deeply affectionate pictures and to whom he was so devoted, was never in his house.

"I would like so much to do something for her," he confided to me. "She is such a good person. We love each other deeply. Even so, I can't be with her. She gets on my nerves.

"Of course, she means so well. But I can't stand to have

57

anyone get a hold on me. When I don't feel well I tell neither Inger nor my housekeeper. I don't want to lie there like a log while they fuss around me.

"'Eat now Edvard,' they say. 'I know you will do it. Lie still, Edvard. No, no—don't be so restless. Have you taken your temperature? Wrap this woolen sock around your neck, won't you? Oh, now you have been painting right here in your bedroom! I can smell it. Let me clean up here—really clean up, I mean. How can you stand to live in this mess? Don't you want me to move in with you? You know I'd be glad to.'

"She means so well, but it doesn't work. Do you know, a few years ago she wanted to publish an illustrated book about our Oslo river—Akerselva—and don't you suppose she waded into the river to her knees to get the best perspectives on her pictures. They were good too; she has a fine sense of surfaces. But I couldn't imagine people standing in line to buy a book about Akerselva. Her publisher planned it as a major work—soft paper and leather binding. From me he wanted original etchings and ten thousand *kroner*—for a major work, you know.

"'You may have twelve hundred,' I said, but twelve hundred was nothing.

"No, I can't stand to have her in the house," he continued. "I have told her not to come and not to call me up. But I do call her. Every week I call Mr. Syversen, the grocer, who lives in the same house. 'Is this Mr. Syversen?' I say. 'This is Munch. Have you seen my sister Inger lately? Does she look all right? Tell her I have called and that I'll send her a package. What do you think she wants—eggs or apples?'"

He helped his brother's daughter, too, and *her* children; answered their letters, but never wanted any member of his family in the house.

"I've got to get going with my painting. I can't take care of children—can't see to it that they have decent shoes and no holes in their pants."

For Inger he established a trust fund of one hundred thousand *kroner*, but admonished her to be frugal: "You must be careful, we're really quite poor. It's true that we can get a good deal of money for *The Frieze of Life,* but you know I'll never let it out of my sight. Really, I hardly have a single picture I can sell, so be careful now; remember I've told you."

In a note to her, he said:

"Dear Inger, when I see you I get tense. And when you see that, you become tense too. That, in turn, makes me more tense than ever. So it is best that we don't see each other any more."

During his last six and a half years Edvard Munch had the same housekeeper, while Inger, his only close relative, was admitted only twice to Ekely.

To his niece Edvard Munch said:

"Be careful. Tell your husband not to go into business. I know his father was an able businessman, but I don't think that's enough reason for your husband to go into business. I cannot take on the expense."

Once he showed me some flower pictures his sister Inger had painted, and I was interested in buying one of them.

"No, please don't buy any. Inger is so excitable. Right now she does nothing but paint. I don't know how it would be if she were able to sell."

His love for his family found the strangest forms of expression. One day in the 1930's he asked me to bring Inger some flowers.

"Do take some flowers to Inger, won't you? It's her birthday tomorrow, and I'd like to give her some flowers. We are really very fond of each other, Inger and I. Ask her how she is getting along—whether she is well and likes the new apartment. Greet her from me and tell her I'm not well enough to bring the flowers myself."

Miss Inger thanked for the flowers and asked if there was anything seriously wrong with Edvard. I assured her there was nothing. "Tell him I'm well," she said, "except for a slight headache."

When I brought him that message Munch begged me to go back right away and insist to Inger that she have an X-ray taken. "Tell her from me that she must go to a good doctor for a head X-ray. I'll pay for it, of course."

Miss Inger did not want to be X-rayed. Even when Munch himself called on her and told her it was his brotherly duty to take care of her and that she would have to go to a doctor, she balked. Then he threatened to cut off all assistance. If she didn't want to listen to him she'd better be entirely on her own. At long last she did go, and Munch received the plates and a letter from the doctor indicating that everything was all right.

"I tell you, I'm so fond of my sister—you know that, of course. Actually, I have had quite a bit of headache myself lately."

All his life Edvard Munch had great power over women. That he was reserved and quiet only made him seem more exciting and mysterious. Many of the most attractive women around had their eyes on him, but he would never commit himself to marriage. Whenever a degree of intimacy developed he was quick to pull out—he simply fled.

When he was poor and lived in considerable discomfort he could have married a woman of means. She is portrayed in some of his erotic canvases. However, when his relationship with her tended to take him away from his work he left her. Ever after, he remained afraid of her.

"You can imagine how she keeps talking about me. I'm sure I know who is behind all this gossip. She'll never forgive me."

In Berlin in the 1890's he became part of a curious quadrangle. We remember his painting *Jealousy*—the nude woman and the green-faced man. One of Munch's friends, a Polish poet named Stanislaus Przybyszewsky, was married to a Norwegian woman whom Munch had known since childhood. Fascinating and beautiful, she was also uninhibited and alluring. Edvard Munch and August Strindberg, regular guests in her home for a period of time, were in love with her, each in his own peculiar way. Munch painted her portrait, which shows her standing like a dark cross on a spotted surface, smiling, her eyes half closed. The portrait brings to mind the painting variously called *Madonna, Woman in the Act of Love,* or *The Conception.* However, it is necessary to see the two side by side to discover the resemblance, see the recapitulation of the linear theme. The same portrait haunts the important canvas entitled *Woman in Three Stages.* Dagny Przybyszewsky is in all of these, but perhaps most notably in the mature woman, the nude, sprawling figure standing with her arms lifted, her hands behind her neck, demonstratively displaying her seductive feminity.

"I don't understand that my nerves didn't cave in back in my Berlin days," he said. "I sat at the table with these people and couldn't say a word. Strindberg talked and talked. All the time I kept thinking, 'Doesn't her husband understand a thing? First he ought to become green with jealousy, then blow his top.'"

Thus, Munch painted the husband green, but rightly he should have put himself or Strindberg into the picture, for the Polish poet, insisting that every person had a free choice in life, that no one could own another human being, was not jealous at all. Once, when his wife wanted to offer herself to a Russian prince the poet himself brought her to her new friend while Munch and Strindberg raged with jealousy. Strindberg wrote: "What do you do to a married woman who in the same week allows herself to be mounted by men from four different countries?"

Her last lover furnished the answer. When she wanted to leave him he shot and killed her.

A few years after the Berlin episode, Edvard Munch traveled from Oslo to Germany in the company of a beautiful and talented woman artist, heiress to a sizeable fortune. Their plan was to live together in Berlin. Already on the train she called Munch her "alter ego" and began to talk about marriage. During a brief stop at a small Swedish station Munch left the train, and for the remainder of the journey the woman was on her own while Munch returned to Oslo.

It was in the 1930's that Munch invited a girl who had

often posed for him to come out to Ekely an evening. He appeared in his best suit, had prepared an attractive table, and served salmon and champagne. After dinner he asked her to step into the bedroom to undress. A few minutes later he appeared in the doorway, looked at her, and said:

"I'm just going to sketch a few lines."

He brought out some charcoal and started to draw. "Now I'll add a few colors." Standing there in his best suit, he painted until he became tired. Then he said:

"Thank you so much. It was nice of you to come."

All Munch's relationships with women—and there were quite a few—were of short duration. Not one does he remember with anything resembling gratitude or pleasure. The more tenderly he was treated, the more frightened he became. In his opinion, women were engaged in an eternal chase to capture lovers and husbands. They *lived* on men—were like leeches and had "nutracker muscles" in their thighs. He portrayed them as mystic and dangerous creatures—women vampires sucking the blood of their helpless victims. The bloody erotic battle of his youth, resulting in the loss of part of his finger, evoked all his latent anxiety. Even women appearing gracious and sweet, he said, were in reality dangerous beasts. All that was necessary to have them show their claws was to reduce the time one spent with them.

"If you only knew how they're whispering and gossiping about me. They hate me because I concentrate on my work and stay unmarried. They feel duped and cheated."

It took a strong man to survive in a marriage, he said. Most husbands cracked under the burden—or at least had their willpower seriously reduced. Of a friend who had entered the marital state he said:

"In a few months he was nothing but soup—it was as if she had extracted all his teeth.

"'Come here,' she'd say, and he came. 'Let's go now,' she'd say, and he would go.

"The entire man was nothing but soup. You had to drag him away from her embrace—he lay there somewhere between her breasts. She was terrible, and his eyes were empty and ashen."

Edvard Munch has described sexual intercourse as woman's mating process with death. Men who live with women, he felt, kill something of themselves.

"The difference between men and women is as great as between round and straight lines. A man living exclusively for his woman loses something of his own characteristics—becomes slippery and round. He can no longer be trusted. But a woman, under the same circumstances, becomes rounder and more feminine.

"After intercourse a man is tired, while a woman wants to talk. The man becomes ashen—his eyes weak and empty, the woman warm and glowing. It is only when a man *leaves* a woman that she collapses. Then it is her turn to have empty eyes and an ashen expression."

Men who married were primarly concerned with food and clothing. They betrayed the world as the priests did —fold your hands—think of heaven.

Munch liked to paint nudes. His women have beautiful, succulent forms, but their faces are often plain and ugly —even frightening. A vision he has often portrayed is a nude woman standing by a bed. In some of the pictures her body is attractive—posed in a flood of light against a dark, spotted wall. In most of them, however, she is ugly and finished despite her youth. Her position is the same in all these pictures—she is moving away from a bed, her head bowed, arms limply at the sides, her hair covering her face—these are the things he remembers.

Another erotic picture he painted particularly often is called *Marat's Death. He* lies bloody and lifeless on the bed—*she* stands there, alluring, hiding the dagger, her face toward the viewer.

The House of Pleasure—to Munch this was filled with fear and horror, blood and murder. He painted many pictures from brothels—all saturated with anxiety and totally devoid of pleasure.

In his later years he also painted male nudes. This he had never done before. And he liked to do self-portraits in the nude. In one of these, a picture from his youth, the painter stands lonely in a dark room—his body afire, his face contorted—he is in hell.

Very many of Munch's pictures center around death. The spirit which drove him to paint the relationship between man and woman also forced him to paint death — his fear of death reflecting his fear of woman. He suffered from an emotional conflict—a tug of war between longing and anxiety—which he felt for the first time in his relationship with his father. Throughout his life Munch felt strongly drawn toward something he both craved and feared—fearing that which motivated his longing.

His tendency toward asceticism may also explain his chronic fear of death.

"I've got to be careful—simply have to use thick boots and be warmly dressed. I can't go around like an athlete and get wet feet. If I do my bronchitis will act up. You have no idea how I have had to fight that bronchitis. I can't sleep with my windows open—day and night I have to be on my guard against bronchitis."

71.6° was the room temperature he preferred. A thermometer was hanging in a string on his bed post, right by his pillow.

"It's such a bother, really. As soon as it slides below seventy I have to get up and fix the furnace—otherwise my bronchitis will show up."

He liked to lie down for a brief rest as soon as he felt tired—but it was not good to lie still too long. It was all right to sleep but dangerous to doze.

To let him know that he did not look well, or that he was pale, was ill advised. Then he would pace the floor restlessly or go and lie down. It was also bad to tell him that you had met someone who looked exceptionally well. This, he thought, was a hint that there was something wrong with *him*. When he learned that Erik Werenskjold had died he said:

"Imagine that—now he's dead too. Everybody always told me, 'Have you seen Werenskiold? You wouldn't believe how well he looks—it's really remarkable.' Yes, that's what they used to tell me. So he died in his sleep, he did. Oh well, I suppose he had gotten old and tired and a bit listless."

He could not stand to see the sick and the old. "Why should that sick old man want to come out here and visit with me?" he asked me once when someone had expressed a wish to see him. "Please, call him up and tell him I am so old myself now that I can't see anyone."

Munch, wanting to know *how* people died, asked me, when my brother passed away:

"Was he in pain? Did he say anything? Was he aware of the fact that he was dying? Was he afraid? Or did he reflect some sort of brightness—as if he had a vision? Or was everything in darkness? Did he have chills? Was he in pain? Do you think people might die simply from pain? Did he get injections? How many? Did he believe in anything? Do you think it helps if you believe?"

Munch, evidently unable to believe in anything transcendental, did not want to rot away, become gas and crumbs. He *hoped* death was a transition into a new existence, but had seen too much spiritual and physical need to be able to believe in God. There would have to be some other meaning to death—something he could not comprehend.

"I wonder what a dog thinks of his master? Does a dog understand anything? Does it believe that we humans are almighty and all-knowing? Even if there is no God, we certainly have nothing to lose by living as if there might be one. He who sows goodness reaps goodness. That I do believe. No, on second thought, I'm not sure of that either. Not always.

"There's something hollow about preachers. You notice it when they chant before the altar. The way they pronounce words of scripture they sound like incantations. Amen, amen. Open sesame. Most preachers are skinny and gray. Heavy, juicy preachers apparently believe more strongly in grace, thinking something like this: 'God will forgive me if I only keep believing in Him.' Maybe they're right too. What do I know?

"Death is pitch black. Colors and light are one. To be a painter is to work with rays of light. To die—perhaps that's like having your eyes poked out. You can't see anymore—perhaps like being thrown into a cellar. Everyone has left you. They have slammed the door shut and gone away. You can't see a thing—you feel only the clammy odor of death itself. There's no light."

It is *The Odor of Death* Munch tried to paint in a picture of his mother which shows a little child who has turned her back on a corpse. His mother lies there pale and thin—he leaves her, holding his nose.

In 1919, while he was still sick, he painted a self-portrait entitled *In the Spanish Flu*. Sitting in an easy chair covered with a blanket, he looks old and weak, his mouth open as if gasping for breath.

"Do you find it nauseating?" he asked.

"What do you mean?"

"Can't you smell it?"

"Smell what?"

"The odor of death—don't you see I'm on the brink of rotting away?"

This was death—to rot and disintegrate—to be transformed into something loathsome and horrible. And death and the odor of death reminded him of something equally loathsome and horrible, submission to a woman. Death and woman had the same odor.

Under an erotic picture Munch wrote: "They are cradled in the embrace of the waves of life, and the woman's smile is the smile of death." And remember what he said in the poem *Alpha and Omega*—"Bending over her dead body, he is frightened by her expression—it was the same expression she had had that moment in the forest when he loved her the most."

A corpse frightened Munch. His memory of the dead bodies of members of his family was remarkably keen. The smile of death which Munch remembers must be that of his mother. Thus, it is reasonable to assume that Munch's problem with women was rooted in this that he could not lie with a good, smiling woman without recalling his dead mother. This visual memory, then, has spread to other senses—a woman acquired the odor of death. Even certain flowers had the fragrance of death.

Edvard Munch was definitely not fond of flowers. Only on birthdays and at Christmas would he accept them as gifts.

"Why am I getting flowers today?" he would ask apprehensively. "I'm not sick, am I? Don't I look well?"

Then, giving the flowers a quick glance, he would remove the card and say: "Please, take these flowers out of the room. I don't want them to die in here."

He had a particular aversion for hyacinths. Finding a bouquet of them in his living room one evening when we returned from a short walk, he flared up angrily and dashed into the kitchen to scold his housekeeper: "Haven't I told you I want no hyacinths in the house? Who sent me these hyacinths?"

The Recluse

When Munch wanted to converse he preferred to be with one person only. Had he accidentally entered a room where several people were gathered he would remain quiet—and exceptionally courteous, to the extent of bending down to pick up things dropped by other guests, even the younger ones. He always insisted on being the last through a doorway, and when he himself had guests would never sit down until he was certain all his guests were seated. Once, when four persons visited him, he ran out of chairs. Leaving the group for a moment, he quickly returned with an empty crate—and a bottle of champagne. He seated himself on the crate: "May I offer you gentlemen a glass of champagne?"

Had I said or done something he did not approve of he never hesitated to let me know. Should anyone happen to approach, however, his tone would change instantly and become pleasant and friendly. He would never sit down until he had offered me a chair.

As the sensitive individual he was, he reacted strongly to words and episodes he did not like. Such matters would penetrate deeply and affect him for years—especially if, somehow, they seemed to reflect on his mental stability. An episode that took place at his house in Hvitsten illustrates his sensitivity in this regard.

Arriving there unannounced one evening, he caught sight of someone walking across his property.

"Who was that walking across my property right now?" he asked the caretaker.

"No one has walked across your property," the caretaker replied.

"What do you mean? I saw two people, dressed in black.

They walked across the property and came from your house."

"There has been no one in my house today," the caretaker insisted, "and no one has walked across the property."

Munch did not stay. He returned to Oslo immediately and came up to my house to relate what had happened. "Would you do me the favor of going down there and fire that caretaker?" he asked. "I can't have people around who think I have hallucinations."

I pleaded for the caretaker.

"No," said Munch. "I want to get rid of him. He is a repulsive fellow. Every time I talk to him he wrings his hands—stands there and wrings his hands while I talk to him. Pale, white hands. I don't think he does a thing, really."

"All he is supposed to do is to keep an eye on the house."

"He thinks I *see* things. I can't stand those chalk-white hands of his."

This happened during the days I was assisting him with an exhibit in London. Immediately after the opening a letter arrived indicating that an offer of one thousand pounds had been received for the fifth version of Sick Girl. Delighted at this first sale of a larger canvas in England, he asked me to write for information regarding the prospective buyer. It turned out to be a Norwegian businessman living in London. Munch, having hoped for an English buyer, was so disappointed that he wanted the exhibit closed without delay, and, when the exhibitors demanded that it be kept open Munch contacted the Norwegian legation asking that his pictures be returned to him. In the meantime, the offer for *Sick Girl* was doubled, still to no avail. The exhibit was to be closed, Munch insisted, and the pictures returned. In desperation the exhibitors wrote asking me to intervene. I replied: "Munch is pretty depressed. Keep the exhibit open according to schedule. I will try to get his consent."

Munch learned of this development and called on me.

"Now you have gone too far," he said. "My paintings are none of your business. We'd better separate—you take care of your business and I mine. Those pictures *must* be returned. And that caretaker in Hvitsten, him I'll fire personally."

The next day he called me up:

"I just sent you a painting—the one of Karl Johan Street that you like so well. What I said yesterday, still goes. You take care of your business and I mine. By the way, there's something I'd like to know. Have they turned off the electricity out here?"

"No, I'm sure they haven't."

"Hm, that's peculiar—there's no electricity here. Get a taxi and come out and take a look at it, will you?"

The electricity was on, of course. It was only that Munch was so afraid of touching the plugs. If anyone had happened to pull out a cord he would never plug it in again himself. I took care of it.

He was bringing some apples to a boil to make fruit soup and remained in the kitchen while he talked about his problems:

"I've had a letter from my niece in Nordland. Now she wants to send her children to Oslo to study. She is asking me whether I feel they ought to continue their schooling or not." He shook his head. "How should I know? I can't answer that question. I surely can't have them here. How would I be able to paint with a house full of youngsters? I'm sure she plans to send them to me, though. What does she mean asking *me* whether she ought to send them to Oslo or not? I'll send her a thousand kroner and tell her I don't want to be involved."

He fished around in the kettle for an apple and brought it over to me. "Here, have an apple," he said, and put it in my hand.

It was boiling hot and I dropped it instantly. He looked at me: "Don't you like apples?"

"It was boiling hot."

"Of course—I didn't think of that." He looked at the apple which lay on the floor smashed to pieces.

"It's dangerous to keep it there. It'll be as slippery as a dance floor—we've got to remove it before I break my neck."

I helped him clean up but couldn't get all of it removed and wanted to get a cloth.

"No, no—don't rub it. Leave it alone. We'll go into the living room."

We went into the adjoining room and he continued to talk about his problems. A sudden thought came to him. "The electricity in the kitchen," he said, "it's on. Would you go out there and turn it off for me?"

I was on my way to the kitchen but was stopped by Munch: "Watch out for that apple. You do remember there's an apple on the floor, don't you?"

Munch rarely attended theatre performances or concerts. If he did go he preferred a front seat next to the aisle. As a rule, he arrived late and left before the performance was over.

"I can't sit still forever," he said.

When some foreign opera stars performed in Oslo during the 1930's he asked me to buy his favorite seat for each day of the performance. Then the second day he called and said: "Don't buy anymore tickets. I went yesterday to hear *Tosca*. The singing was fine, I thought, but the sets were awful. Exactly the same as thirty years ago. You know, I think the sets I painted for Max Reinhardt thirty years ago would have appeared brand new even today. Why does everything seem to change except theatre painting?"

Shortly after my brother had passed away Munch asked me to come out to Ekely. As soon as I arrived he said:

"You must forgive me for not attending your brother's funeral. I only sent a wreath. I can't stand such things. The last funeral I went to was my sister's. It took me a long time to get over it.

"What am I saying? Since I didn't even know your

brother I don't suppose it would have been that hard on me. Really, though, it's true that I never go to funerals. When my cousin Edvard Didriks died I went as far as to the crematory. But I didn't go in—stayed in the car. I saw the smoke—thick and yellow."

One of Oslo's most active art dealers in the 1930's was Oscar Johannessen. Originally short of money and even shorter on professional training, he had nevertheless worked himself up to considerable prominence. Having no gallery or shop he bought and sold in rapid sequence.

"I don't claim to know anything about art," he said. "All I know is what people want and what I can get for a picture. It must not be too large, that makes it difficult to sell. It has to fit above a buffet or a desk. If it's an Askevold painting people want cows in it, and in a Thaulow running water is a must. A painting by Munch ought to resemble Christian Krohg's work. Whenever I'm in doubt I ask my wife; then we hit people's taste right on the button."

After many attempts, Johannessen finally succeeded in being admitted into Munch's presence. He came to buy pictures. When I met the dealer the next day he related his experiences at Ekely:

"No, sir. That Munch is a difficult one. He talked one streak but never a word about pictures. I accomplished nothing. Can't you help me get some Munch pictures? I have lots of buyers."

The next time I called on the artist I told him that Johannessen was very interested in buying.

"That's right. He was out here. It was really embarrassing. He talked and talked. I couldn't get a word in."

An art dealer came up to me with three Munch pictures one day. I thought they looked familiar and asked the dealer to wait while I talked to Munch on the telephone. It turned out to be three pictures stolen from the garden at Ekely. The dealer had bought them from the thief, a young man. I brought the pictures out to Munch. The entire episode upset him very much.

"What if he kills himself?" he worried. "He is just a young man, the son of prominent people. Please, tell him I do not intend to prosecute. Tell him from me that no one will be told. Tell him also that the pictures were no good. They've had one "horse cure" after the other —must have stood out there in the garden for months and gotten worse and worse."

Far from contemplating suicide, the young man put on an air of impudence and insisted that Munch had given him the pictures.

This brought Munch to the point of exasperation. He wiped his forehead continuously and moaned: "This is terrible. Either we drive him from pillar to post until he kills himself—for the sake of those miserable pictures —or he'll get people to believe him. Of course, most people will believe him—assume that he has been posing for me or something like that. Then he'll steal everything he wants around here and say, 'I keep getting pictures from Munch. We're such good friends, you know.'

"No, I'd better move down to Hvitsten. I can't live here. Barbed wire and mad dogs don't seem to help in the least. No, really, I can't stand to live here. People peer into the garden when I take a stroll. Damn it, this property is situated so low. Everything people empty out in the houses higher up trickles down to me. Up there it's quite dry while I have to wade around in their refuse." He mopped his brow.

"Now they've gotten something new to gossip about —'Imagine Munch giving one picture after the other to this young man! Isn't that something—Munch giving him one picture after the other.'

"Now they'll be whispering left and right. Soon I'll have the whole pack at my heels. You know, they've just complained that my house is not villa-like—it ruins the value of their lots, they say. I spoil the entire neighborhood with these simple frame structures. Well, well, now the Oslo mob will get grist to their mill. I won't get a moment's peace."

He did go to Hvitsten to stay for a while. When I came

down to see him a Sunday afternoon he complained about a prominent man from Oslo who kept visiting him.

"I saw him on Karl Johan and, on a sudden impulse, wanted to paint him. So I went over and asked if he wanted to pose for me. 'Gladly', he said.

"Now he comes every day and sits in that chair in front of me, and I can't get started with my painting. We talk and talk and finally he says: 'Aren't you going to paint?'

"'Paint', I say. 'Yes, weren't you going to paint a portrait of me? I don't think I have time to come down here anymore.'

"Finally, he picked up his hat and left. But by that time he had told me everything he had done in his entire lifetime. I'm sure he felt that the Grand Cross of the Order of St. Olav, which I got, should really have gone to him instead."

Sitting there explaining to me how hopelessly difficult it was to get started on a work of art, Munch began to carve a piece of wood. Talking and carving—concentrating with increasing eagerness on the work at hand—he did not remove his eyes from the piece of wood. I had no idea what he was developing and was quite surprised when it turned out to be a portrait of me.

Just before I left, Munch's caretaker came running. "A boat has capsized right outside the point," he said. "There's a young boy in it."

"Wouldn't you know it," Munch exclaimed. "Now he has sailed down here to get revenge—has drowned himself right in front of my property. There will be investigations and trials and all sorts of racket."

He looked at me coldly and continued: "Why did you drag me into this mess? Hauling those stolen pictures back to me, dragging me into this damn business. Did I need those miserable pictures? Didn't you see they were no good?"

It was a local boy who had capsized. He straightened up his boat, bailed it out and made it to shore safely.

"What a dismal hole this Hvitsten is," Munch exclaimed. "When the youngsters around here don't know what to do they take up capsizing in front of my property. Frankly, it would be better if they stayed home and took up drinking—with moderation, of course. Then, perhaps, I could work in peace."

Slowly his mood changed, he became warm and mischievous.

"Have you met my innkeeper?" he asked; "the one who owns Hvitsten Inn? You've got to see his collection. Let's have a look at Krogvik's collection."

Krogvik bowed deeply when we arrived.

"This is a young art collector from Oslo," Munch said. "He'd like very much to see your collection. There's no one in this country who has that many pictures of Peter Spurvik. They are by Spurvik, aren't they?" Munch added, pronouncing the name of the unknown amateur as if he were a classic.

"I should rather have bought a picture by you, sir," the innkeeper said. "One Munch picture would be worth much more than all of the pictures I have. I suppose it's too late to buy now?"

"That's true, I'm afraid. They give me a thousand *kroner* for my foot print these days. When I get wet feet all I have to do is to place them on a piece of cardboard, and I make a thousand *kroner*."

"I hear that rich people in Oslo buy Munch paintings paying thousands upon thousands of *kroner* for them," the innkeeper continued.

"No, that's not so," Munch replied with sudden vehemence. "Don't get the idea that I sell paintings. Come up to my house some day, and you'll see that I keep all of them. It's only hearsay that I sell paintings—it's graphic works I sell."

Munch had no desire to be rich, nor did he care to associate with rich people. In the 1920's he went to Paris with his friend Halfdan Rode, noted Norwegian opera singer, and Rode's wife and daughter. The Rodes took rooms in a fashionable hotel while Munch rented a simple room facing the backyard of an apartment building. He did not stay long.

"I don't like the people here," he complained. "I can't paint and live in such a fancy room."

In Paris he painted a portrait of Miss Rode. In the course of the sittings she decided to change her hairdo.

"What have you done to yourself?" Munch burst out. "You have become a completely different person."

One could not remain Munch's friend and associate with people *he* did not like. He might break up a friendship if he as much as saw the other party stand on the sidewalk talking to such a person.

"Now I caught him," he would say. "I've suspected this for a long time. He stood there talking to Søren —gossiping probably. And he has assured me he can't stand Søren."

It was Søren Onsager, painter and director of the National Gallery, whom Munch disliked so strongly.

Strange to say, Munch actually craved to learn to know people, wanted to feel close to them, learn to know their deepest secrets. All the same, he established no bonds. He did not dare—perhaps because, in reality, he wished so much to do it. He protected himself by saying that man was untrustworthy and evil. He was hiding something when he pretended there was a plot against him and suddenly found it necessary to get away. In reality he was fleeing from an overpowering desire to be near people. Under these circumstances he *had* to leave. Entirely without plans, without baggage, and with no definite idea where he was going, he would board a train. Once, on such a sudden trip—it was on the Stockholm train—he met the Swedish painter Isaac Grünewald.

"What are you planning to do in Stockholm?" Grünewald asked.

"I'm just traveling a little—I sleep so much better on the train."

Halfdan Christensen, director of Oslo's National Theatre, met Munch once on the train to Gothenburg in Sweden. Munch had boarded in Moss, thirty miles south of Oslo. Christensen was spending only one day in

Gothenburg, and he and Munch happened to take in at the same hotel.

Christensen, entering the dining room, found Munch alone at dinner and joined him and in the course of the conversation asked Munch what he was doing in Gothenburg.

"I have been to the movies," he replied. "That's all I have done here. I simply had to get away from Oslo —even took a steamer from Skøyen to Moss to avoid traveling through the city."

They sat talking until four o'clock in the morning, the time Christensen's train left for Oslo. When the theatre director rose to leave, Munch left also. Seeing Christensen buy a first class ticket, however, Munch decided on second class. He left the train in Moss.

Munch and his pictures

In all Munch's houses—in Aasgaardstrand, Hvitsten, and Ekely—there were unfinished canvases and completed paintings. It is doubtful that any other great artist has collected his own works as eagerly as Munch did. He was very reluctant to sell a painting he liked and, even more so, one he did not like. If, to provide money, he had found it necessary to sell a painting he was fond of, he was ill at ease until he had painted the same subject over again. He wanted his own collection to contain all his principal works.

"I have no other children than these pictures," he would say. "To be able to continue working I must have them around me—just a look at them is enough to get me going again. If I'm away from these children I do little more than sketching. If I send them away to major exhibits I descend to the low level of a restless and vain newspaper reader. It's impossible for me to resist reading what they say about my pictures, although I know it's dangerous. Praise is particularly dangerous. I know I have to develop. Praise is paralyzing—someone stands behind you whispering: 'Keep painting this way and that way —then you'll be praised!'

"I've never had time for marriage. When I was young I couldn't afford it. Instead, I have always been loyal to the Goddess of Art, and she has stayed by me."

Whatever Munch possessed of strength and ability he devoted exclusively to his painting. Had he believed he would become a better painter by standing on his head a few minutes every day he would undoubtedly have done so. His pictures are rarely pleasant, his drawings never neat—model likeness is secondary—his works reflect his own soul.

Once he received the distinct honor of being asked to paint a portrait of a member of the royal house. He declined: "I'm too old to paint medals."

Nevertheless, when Prince Eugene of Sweden, a distinguished painter and an untiring champion of Scandinavian art, celebrated his seventieth birthday, Munch sent this cable: "In gratitude for your noble efforts in the kingdom of the arts."

It happened that Munch simply manhandled his pictures. He might fly at them in a rage, kick them, tear them apart.

"That damn picture gets on my nerves—I've given it one "horse cure" after the other, but it keeps getting worse and worse. Do me the favor of taking it up to the attic. Just toss it in there—as far in as possible."

I brought it up but was unable to open the attic door and had to leave the picture in the hallway.

"Did you get the door open?" he asked when I came down again.

"No."

Munch dashed upstairs, tore open the door and flung the picture into the darkness. "It's an evil child—I've tried everything with it, but it resists my efforts. Believe me, that picture—if I hadn't locked it in there—would have been capable of jumping down from the hallway and hitting me in the head. Really, I've got to get it out of the house—it's a terrible picture."

He dropped down in a chair and wiped his brow.

"Nothing seems to turn out right anymore."

He kicked another picture. "That one is poor too. Take it away. Hands I have never been able to paint. I know perfectly well that I have never been able to paint hands. The director of the National Gallery said this picture was good—he must be out of his mind. People keep writing page upon page of what a great painter I am. Now, what's your honest opinion of that picture?"

I didn't answer.

"I think I'll go down to Hvitsten. I've got to rest a little, and Hvitsten is the only place where I can rest. There isn't a thing down there I'd want to paint. It's a place of perfect rest. In fact, I've thought of moving down there permanently—it's a terribly monotonous hole. I usually go down there on Christmas Eve just to torture myself by working on *Mother Earth*. For twenty years I've been painting *Mother Earth*. Every Christmas Eve I stand down in Hvitsten and paint *Mother Earth* over again. It's raw and chilly down there too, so I'm really atoning for my sins. There's no decent stove in the house—just a useless contraption. Then I walk around in the wet, sticky snow and look across the fjord to Aasgaardstrand . . . ." His voice changed. "You can't turn around in Aasgaardstrand without finding something you want to paint. I've painted everything there is to paint there —trees, houses, stones. I might actually do another painting of the beach with the boulders on it—boulders like living beings. So far I have always had people sitting on the boulders—with the result that I get nothing more than another picture of Jappe Nielsen or Inger sitting on a stone." He became livelier. "You know, I'd really like to go down to Aasgaardstrand and paint a picture of the beach and those boulders—paint them like living beings." But his frustration returned: "No, I'd better go to Hvitsten—I can't stand to paint anymore. Why didn't I go into something else? A big, husky fellow like me sitting here day in and day out with charcoal sticks and little brushes."

Instead of continuing to work on sketches and drafts he had standing around, Munch often started over again. "If I work more on this particular canvas," he would say, "it will begin to smell of sweat." One of his best known paintings, *Mother Earth*—a principal mural in the *Aula* decorations and the one he spoke so disparagingly about —he painted over again twenty times!

Once I offered two thousand *kroner* for a sketch he had standing at Ekely.

"That's a good price for those few lines," he mused. "But I can't sell it—must keep on. It's dangerous to sell sketches. I can't give up that soon."

In a few hours he called me up.

"It's Munch here. I'll let you have that sketch for *one* thousand *kroner*. You remember you offered me *two*. But I'd better warn you—I have worked on it some more. Come out and have a look."

Munch had no mercy on people who tried to tell him how to paint. Standing with him inside the Ekely gate one day, I witnessed the arrival of an artist friend from Munch's early days. He greeted Munch and asked to be let in.

"No. I never let anyone in."

"But you do have company."

"Can't I be allowed to sell a picture without being disturbed?"

"Why don't you let me in for just a moment, Edvard? I'd like so much to see what you are doing."

"Didn't you hear me? I don't want you in here. Don't you remember what happened last time?"

"Have I been here before?"

"Of course, you have. I stood in the garden looking at a white trotter and a old work horse. Holding on to the reins I ran around with the horses a bit—wanted to see how they lifted their legs. 'Well, well, Edvard,' you said, 'so you've become a circus director now?'"

"But it was just a joke."

"I suppose ... but when I showed you that picture I had painted, you asked: 'Why do you use so much green in it?'"

The old friend tipped his hat and left.

"He's among the worst ones," Munch said. "He says he likes my pictures—still he keeps painting like a pedantic old maid."

During the hanging of a new version of *Mother Earth*

in the *Aula,* Munch noticed a worker looking at the murals and approached him with the question: "Well, what do you think of these pictures?"

The worker pointed to the old man in the center of *The History:* "That man has a green beard."

"That's right—he has a green beard."

Munch and the worker stood there looking at each other.

"I asked what you thought of the pictures," Munch persisted.

"There's no such thing as a green beard," the worker said matter-of-factly.

Visibly angered, Munch blurted out: "What the hell are you doing here anyway? Get out!"

A few days later, he asked me to come with him to see the *Aula* decorations. He looked carefully at each of the murals except *Mother Earth,* the only one in the series he was unhappy with. As he walked along the wall where *Mother Earth* is hanging he said:

"Why does there have to be a wall here? Must an auditorium always have four walls? Wouldn't it have been more exciting to have something different right here—a few magnificent tapestries, perhaps? Last night I dreamed I had finally succeeded with *Mother Earth.* It made me so happy I started dancing. Still in the dream, I sat down in a chair and a flock of angels came and took me away ... I'd better go down to Hvitsten and paint *Mother Earth* again. Right before I called you today I sketched those angels."

He felt that *Mother Earth* lacked unity. Initially, wanting to portray children who in their daily play carry out a form of research, he had thought of calling this part of the decorations *Scientists.* In its present form, according to Munch, the left side of the mural tends to disintegrate, it lacks a true function.

A well-to-do businessman asked Munch to paint a portrait of his wife and offered to pay ten thousand *kroner* for it. Munch replied that he would have to see the model before he made up his mind. She came to visit and Munch wanted very much to paint her. The result of the sittings was a fine portrait of a young lady in an airy summer dress. When the picture was turned over to the husband he telephoned Munch and said he liked it, but that the facial features were too vague—the entire head nothing but a mere touch of pink.

"That's what's especially good about it," Munch said. "Your wife doesn't have any features—nothing but the black stuff she smears above her eyes."

Actually, Munch liked the young lady and commented a little later: "That certainly was an airy dress she wore!"

When Munch in 1922 had finished a series of murals for the Freia Chocolate Factory in Oslo the director asked him to add a few touches. The workers had complained of the lack of doors and chimneys in the pictures. Munch did go back to the factory and added a little here and there. The director, noticing that Munch kept a taxi waiting, offered to place one of Freia's own cars at the artist's disposal. One day, when the car was not waiting at its designated place, Munch ran to the director and complained:

"Why do you make me stand here painting all by myself?"

A few days later he came unannounced into the director's office, tossed his brushes on the desk, and said:

"Now you can ruin the rest of it by yourself!"

A Sunday afternoon at Ekely I met Jappe Nielsen. At an art dealer's in Oslo he had seen a picture with Munch's signature but was quite certain Munch had not painted it. A week later, when I met Jappe at Ekely again, the matter was brought up once more. Jappe asked Munch:

"Have you really been down at the dealer's looking at the picture and saying that you have painted it? That's what they told me."

"No, I didn't say that," Munch replied. "What I did say was that it was *possible* I had painted it. Perhaps the woman with her back to the viewer is my sister, I said. What business is that of yours, anyway? I don't want any fuss about it—writing and that sort of thing. Didn't you see that it was a pretty good picture?"

It turned out to be a painting by Harriet Backer, an artist from the transitional period between realism and neo-romanticism, noted particularly for interior motifs in which the interplay between color and light creates a meaningful thematic tension. The Harriet Backer painting, originally sold in Germany, had now arrived back in Norway, complete with Munch's signature!

Only once have I seen Munch willing to pay cash to get back a picture he had sold. A German collector had a Munch painting for sale, and I had received a photo of it.

"You must buy it," Munch urged. "It's probably the best work I have ever done. If you don't do it I'll buy it myself."

"What kind of an offer should we make?"

"Buy it—regardless of the price. I do want it here."

The transaction was completed. Then, when Munch saw the painting his opinion changed:

"Ugh, isn't it better than that! Why don't you try to send it back to Germany. It's a pretty poor picture. And I was so sure it was a good one!"

That's the only time I can recall that Munch's memory seemed to fail in regard to one of his own works.

Munch could be very careless with his paintings, even to the extent of stepping on them when they lay on the floor.

"A good painting can take quite a bit," he said. "Only poor paintings require neatness and gilded frames. As a rule I frame mine with a narrow rim, preferably one that's round and white."

If anyone else took liberties with his works, however, it was a different matter.

"Now Jens Thies has allowed Harald Brun to clean and polish my pictures," he complained once, speaking about the director of the National Gallery and the gallery's technical consultant. "I didn't even recognize a picture I saw—one of my best. He has allowed Harald Brun to retouch it!"

As a precaution against fire hazard, Munch had built several houses at Ekely—one in brick, the others frame structures. Later, these houses were not large enough to accomodate all his works, and he hit on the idea of building a high fence of solid boards from one house to the next, with a narrow roof extending some three feet out from the top of the fence to provide a degree of protection. Under this roof he put up many of his largest pictures. One day, when he asked me what I thought of the fence, I replied:

"It's made of wood. If a fire should start some place it would spread along the fence from one house to the next."

Munch stepped away from me, then turned around, looked at me askance and very disapprovingly said:

"I can't stand to show you my pictures."

I realized then what my comment had done to him and left instantly. More than a month passed before Munch called me again.

Munch always spoke very kindly of those who in his early years had given him a few hundred *kroner* for a picture. If they ran into difficulties he was always willing to help. However, if anyone who had bought a picture inexpensively in the past came to have it signed he usually refused.

"Ten *kroner* is all you paid for it," he might say. "Aren't you happy with the bargain? Perhaps you'd like me to frame it for you?" Yet if he liked the picture he would sign it anyway.

Once he was approached in the street by a lady whose father had bought a painting from him back in the difficult years. Now, her own two children, she told Munch, were arguing about the right to inherit the treasure. "Do you think you might possibly let me buy another so that the children may inherit one each?"

"I remember your father well," Munch replied; "a fine gentleman he was—gave me two hundred *kroner* for the picture although he could easily have gotten it for fifty. It's people like him who make it possible for an artist to make living. Why don't you come home with me, and I'll let you have a picture quite reasonably."

The lady accompanied Munch to Ekely, and he chose a painting for which she paid five thousand *kroner*. Not long after, however, Munch began to worry. What sort of picture had he handed her? All he seemed to remember about it was that it was one he had given several "horse cures"—a poor one, maybe. He telephoned the lady:

"You haven't let anyone see it, have you? Yes, this is Munch. That picture I gave you, it's a poor one. People might think I'm finished as a painter. Please, take a cab right away and bring it back, will you? It's such a poor one—everything happened too fast. I just grabbed a picture that was standing there—can't even remember which one. I'll give you a fine, large one instead; only, do take a cab and bring it back. It's a poor picture."

When she arrived with it Munch mopped his brow: "You haven't shown it to anyone, have you? Well, that was five thousand, wasn't it? Here's your money back. You must give me a little more time and do me the favor of leaving. I can't take care of any more business transactions today."

Undoubtedly, months passed before he found a suitable substitute.

Of one of Oslo's great private collectors, a grand patron of the arts, he said:

"He never calls on me alone—always comes with a host of people. They fuss like all hell. Painters, critics, and even Søren from the Gallery. After they have looked the pictures over they step out into the hallway to *vote*. The collector himself has only one vote like the rest. Of course, it'll always be the picture Søren likes—they keep voting until they all agree on the one Søren likes."

I had made Munch an offer on two pictures he refused to sell, one a winter landscape, the other entitled *Gothic Girl*. Very early one morning he called on me. In my living room I had four paintings by Munch and two by

Karsten. In Munch's opinion, the paintings didn't hang right. We took all of them down and then put only his four up again.

"Now we'll go to my place," he said, "and pick up that winter landscape and the Gothic girl."

We brought the pictures back, and he presented them to me as a gift. Although I wanted to pay for them he refused to accept money.

"No, no—they hang so well and safely here. But you must promise me that you'll find a good place for those Karsten pictures we took down."

One Christmas morning the door bell rang. To the maid who opened the caller said:

"I'm just a poor old painter who has a small picture to sell. Do you think anyone in this house might be interested in having a look at it?"

It was a picture of a dog. Having persistently refused to sell it, he now presented me with it as a Christmas gift.

Shortly after the city of Oslo had announced the names of the artists chosen to decorate the new Town Hall, a prominent citizen approached Munch in the street:

"Well, well, and how are you, Mr. Munch? I was sorry to learn that this great commission didn't go to you."

Munch remained mum.

Then the man tapped him patronizingly on the shoulder: "I'll be out one of these Sundays to buy a picture from you."

"You'd better make sure the country store will be open."

"That man," Munch told me later, "was the one who closed off that last glimpse of the fjord we had from Karl Johan."

"For a long time now I've been wanting to exhibit some colored drawings," Munch said once. "I don't want to sell them, only see them framed and displayed. Perhaps you could take care of that for me?"

I did. There were forty drawings. On seeing them altogether, he said: "They look good. Give me one hundred fifty *kroner* each, and you may keep them."

It meant a great deal to Munch to see his works favorably displayed. Of one picture, which hung particularly well in my house, he said:

"It really ought to go with the house. It belongs where it is right now.

"I've seen one of my pictures share a wall with Van Gogh and Gauguin," he continued. "In Dresden, it was. To be frank, my picture did all right—held its own."

In 1921, Munch painted a new version of *The Dance of Life* to enable me to have that important work in my collection. While he worked on it I spent quite a bit of time with him. Once, wanting to add a touch of blue, he accidentally got some brown paint on his brush, and a streak of that color spotted a surface of water. Greatly upset, he tossed the brush away:

"The picture is ruined. Tomorrow you must have a new canvas delivered—the same measurements, remember!"

"But couldn't you paint over it?"

"I never paint over anything."

"How about scraping it out with a knife,then?"

"No. I don't do that anymore. The picture is ruined."

He put on hat and coat to walk out with me. When we reached the gate he hesitated for a moment: "I might paint a little twig on that brown spot." He pondered a little. "Yes, I could do that, couldn't I? I'll go back in and paint a little twig."

When the picture was finished he asked probingly how I liked it.

"I like it very much," I replied.

"Even that brown twig?"

Later, Jappe Nielsen, Munch's good friend, spoke very highly of the picture.

"You do notice that I have painted a little twig on that tree there, don't you?" Munch asked Jappe. "Do you think it spoils the picture?"

"Not at all, why should it?"

When Jappe had left Munch said: "Poor Jappe—now he's finished as a critic."

Many years thereafter, Munch came to our house one Sunday afternoon. He seemed disturbed—walked restlessly up and down. I walked with him. Suddenly he blurted out: "Can't you sit down! Do you always have to walk up and down like that?"

I sat down and Munch did the same. He sat with his back to the wall where *The Dance of Life* was hanging. I looked at him—casually.

"What are you looking at—my tie, perhaps?"

I lifted my eyes and looked aimlessly at the wall behind him.

"Is it that damn twig you keep looking at? Didn't I tell you to buy a new canvas!"

The executive of one of Oslo's largest business establishments was celebrating his sixtieth birthday. It was in the 1930's. The board members decided to present him with a Munch painting and asked me to help them select a large picture.

The day after the celebration, a delivery man with a cart appeared outside the Ekely gate. The painting the board had purchased was being returned.

Reporting the incident to me, Munch waved his arms in annoyance and agitation:

"If *I* buy my sister a pair of shoes as a gift and she doesn't like them, can she get *my* money back by returning the shoes?"

"No, I shouldn't think so."

"Well, there you see—for art entirely different laws seem to apply. It isn't enough that the *buyer* likes the picture—the recipient has to like it too."

Shortly thereafter, a wealthy land owner wanted to buy a painting. Before completing the transaction, Munch asked the patron:

"You aren't going to give this painting away, are you?"

"Yes, as a matter of fact, I am; it's a gift for my wife."

"Does she have a cart?" Munch asked to the astonishment of the gentleman.

In a review in *Dagbladet,* Jappe Nielsen wrote very

scornfully of a young artist's one-man show. Munch read the review and called up his old friend:

"What's happening to you, Jappe? Why do you write such stuff?"

"Have you seen the show?" Jappe countered.

"No, I haven't, but I know that no one ought to write as insultingly as that about a young artist. If there's something in his works you don't like or don't understand you might indicate that. You might say, 'These paintings I don't understand' or 'These pictures had nothing to give me.' Don't you see? You, of all people, should have learned something from *my* experiences."

"Do you want me to quit writing, then?"

"No, by no means. Keep on. You write well about pictures you like."

"But Edvard, I can't keep writing only about you, can I?"

"What about icons?" Munch suggested. "You do like icons, don't you? Why not write something about them?"

Munch remembered all of his pictures and tried to keep track of their whereabouts. In his later years, he often painted several versions of the same picture. Then he would keep the one he liked best. "It forms part of *The Frieze of Life,*" he would say. "I couldn't possibly sell it."

His graciousness toward those who had bought pictures from him in his difficult years was not reflected in his attitude toward later buyers. This is illustrated by a telephone conversation he had with a shipowner who in the 1930's had purchased a painting for the considerable sum of thirty thousand *kroner:*

"This is Munch. I miss that painting I sold you and would like to borrow it for a while. I need it to paint another version for my own collection."

"You may come to my house and have a look at it any time you feel the urge," the shipowner replied.

"That won't do," Munch said. "I want it here. After all, the picture is actually mine. To buy a painting is not like buying a piece of brick, you know. All you do is to buy the right to keep it in your house. That's why I had to charge you so much, otherwise you might not have bothered taking proper care of it."

Munch consented to do a portrait of the daughter of a Bergen shipowner. When it was finished, however, the shipowner refused to accept it.

"She looks terrible," he said.

"That's right," Munch agreed. "She is both ugly and temperamental, but don't you think the picture is good?"

Munch had no objection when critics and dealers furnished his pictures with titles. He preferred those of literary connotations—*Two People, The Meeting, The Kiss, Ocean of Love, The Dance of Life, Solace, Vampire, Marat's Death, Ashes.* That many of his paintings have several names has already been noted in reference to the one called *Woman in the Act of Love* which is also known as *Conception* and *Madonna,* the last title furnished by Jens Thiis of the National Gallery when the work became a part of the Munch collection there. If someone had suggested calling it *Erotic Waves* Munch would undoubtedly have accepted that title as well. What mattered to him was that a picture had a subject title. Abstract terms like *Composition in Red* or *Landscape in Blue* did not appeal to him.

Once we previewed one of his exhibits and came across a print of a woman's face.

"Who sat for that?" I asked.

"I don't remember her name," Munch replied. "But she did have a fine face—like ancient nobility."

"Maybe it should be entitled *The Countess.*"

"That's perfect," he replied enthusiastically. "Although I don't remember her name I do remember who she was —the madam of a brothel in Lübeck. Who knows, she might have been a countess at that!"

Sales and Collections

Of his best-known work, *Sick Girl,* Munch painted at least six versions. Although always using the same size canvas, he varied brush strokes and colors considerably from one version to the next. The first, dated 1886 and now in the Munch Room of the National Gallery, is more gray in tone than subsequent ones. The second, painted in 1896, now in Gothenburg Museum of Art in Sweden, was part of the National Gallery collection until replaced by the older version. The third, dated 1906, is in Stockholm's Thiel Collection, while a fourth is in the Art Gallery of Dresden.

The fifth version Munch sold in 1920 to a private collector in Norway for fifty thousand *kroner,* a record price for a Norwegian work of art. Shortly after the sale, however, he had second thoughts about it and succeeded in getting the picture back in exchange for two other canvases. Although dated 1926, the sixth version, I suspect, was painted somewhat earlier. Knowing Munch's deep affection for this particular subject, I feel rather certain he must have painted the sixth version soon after the sale of the fifth, i.e., already in 1920, prior to the return of the fifty thousand *kroner* canvas. Thus, the exchange transaction completed, he was left with two versions in his own collection.

Personally, I have seen only six versions of *Sick Girl,* but Pola Gauguin claims there are eight. In all probability, Munch painted this subject at least once every ten years, perhaps to check on his own artistic development at such widely spaced but regular intervals. In addition, he may have produced two canvases to fill immediate gaps in his own collection.

The large painting *Springtime,* now in the National Gallery, was purchased shortly after its completion in 1889 by a friend who offered one hundred *kroner* for it but never bothered to pick it up!

His 1889 picture of Hans Jaeger, literary spokesman for the Oslo Boheme, suffered a similar destiny. The portrait, by Munch himself considered a failure, shows Jaeger as many remembered him: a frail and hunched up man glumly seated at the Bohemian group's table at the Grand. But it was certainly not in that negative pose Munch wanted his friend, the great humanitarian seeker, remembered.

"Hans Jaeger was one of the finest men I have ever met," he said with great emphasis, "a thoroughly honest person."

That two of his friends, Sigurd Bødtker and Jappe Nielsen, liked the picture when it was first shown surprised Munch very much. "In that case," he said, "you may give me enough money for paint and a new canvas and keep the picture—give me six *kroner.*"

His friends did not accept the offer.

Munch's ardent supporter Jens Thiis, director of the National Gallery, also liked Jaeger's portrait, much to Munch's displeasure.

"That picture is not very representative of me," he complained. "For that reason it shouldn't be in the National Gallery. Christian Krohg could have painted it—in fact, anyone could have painted it."

Until his fortieth year Munch had a difficult time selling his pictures. Canvases from his early period might bring a few hundred *kroner,* but those from *The Frieze of Life* and others from his best years were not much in demand. Even so, he would rather go hungry than change his style and manner to please prospective buyers.

His first major change in technique and subject matter dates from the year 1908, but the public's attitude toward his works remained unaffected by the change. The demand for his moody, pessimistic pre-1908 pictures was on a steady increase while his new and brighter works remained largely ignored. Even after he rose to world fame, attention seemed to focus entirely on his early works.

In the dating of his pictures, Munch is curiously unreliable. In his later period, he might add a few brush strokes to paintings that had been standing around for many years and then supply such works with very recent dates. On the other hand, paintings completed in the 1930's might be given dates going ten to fifteen years back.

"Of course, I realize that I painted that picture right now," he would say when questioned about it. "However, I've had it ready in my mind for a long time—actually, it's probably fifteen years since I first sketched it. The fact is, I haven't had time to finish it until now. So it ought to be marked '1906—1908.'"

Munch lived in critical financial circumstances for a long time. Once, an aquaintance offered him ten *kroner* to do a portrait of a relative laid out in his casket.

"It was a gruesome experience," he recalled with a shudder. "I was thinking the corpse might stir—say something, perhaps. What could I possibly have answered? Yet I had to have that money."

When he attended his own brother's funeral a close relative approached him with a plea:

"Why don't you paint something people will buy, Edvard? I know perfectly well you can do it. When you think of it, it's really inconsiderate of you, especially when you know so well how poor we all are."

From 1908 and on, as the demand for his paintings increased, his prices rose accordingly. Much credit for this change must go to Ernst Thiel, Swedish art patron and connoisseur who in 1906, when Munch was poor and on the brink of a nervous breakdown, purchased six paintings and more than fifty graphic works—truly a royal gesture. In a Thiel portrait, for which Munch received six thousand *kroner,* he pictured his benefactor as a Semitic prince in northern attire.

In 1908, Munch sold five paintings to the National Gallery in Oslo. Although the asking price was thirty thousand *kroner* he received only ten thousand. Under the circumstances, however, it was a favorable sale for Munch, and also for the Gallery administration whose financial conservatism had been considerably tempered by the Thiel purchase.

Now Munch's prints also began to command impressive prices. Already in 1911, a color lithograph of *Sick Girl* brought twelve hundred *kroner.*

Prior to World War I, Munch's works went primarily to German collectors and galleries. During the war, however, when Scandinavian neutrality created a financial boom, particularly in the shipping field, his market at home rose rapidly. In the years 1916 to 1920, it was not uncommon for Munch to receive thirty thousand *kroner* for a painting. His prints, of which he sold thousands, brought two or three hundred *kroner,* while those he decided to hold back soared to prices unheard of for graphic works. Thus, in 1920 a print of *Sick Girl* was sold for four thousand *kroner.* Munch's annual sales in those years averaged four hundred thousand *kroner!*

Although he liked to sell prints he made certain each edition was relatively small. Lithographs and etchings were usually printed in one hundred copies. *Sick Girl* and *Madonna* have appeared in several editions of one hundred copies each. His woodcuts appeared in a minimum of ten and a maximum of thirty copies. Because Munch, unlike most artists, failed to keep count of his prints no one knows exactly how many he made and sold. However, it is reasonable to assume that more than fifty thousand copies have been produced, and that close to thirty thousand of these were sold in Germany alone. His earliest prints, of which Munch himself kept very few, now bring from three or four thousand *kroner* each.*

* In 1966 a color lithograph of *Madonna* sold in Switzerland for 120,000 Swiss Francs, *i.e.,* $30,000.00.

Munch found it beneath his dignity as an artist to carry on commercial activities. Consequently, he was always ill at ease when first approached about a sale. In reality, however, he possessed a well-developed sense of the value of money and ultimately became a master salesman. A person having succeeded in buying a picture from Munch was left with the unmistakable impression of having had a great favor bestowed upon him. Munch told the prospective buyer—and he was merely stating the truth—that he found it neither necessary nor to his liking to sell his works. If the buyer then expressed interest in a particular picture the artist would never quote a price. Instead, he waited for the buyer to make an offer. If Munch found it too low he would simply not sell the picture. An acceptable offer, on the other hand, might prompt this response:

"Do you have the money on hand? Well then, if you want to pay that much you may take it with you."

Quickly, without counting, he would stuff the bills in his pocket.

"I'm sure I have lost thousands by not counting," he said, "but I can't make myself do it—at least not while people are watching."

As a rule, he signed his pictures only at the time of the sale. I have seen him moved to tears as he put his signature on a canvas. "Well, well"—and he would sigh deeply—"now that one will be lost—I suppose I'll never see it again."

In his later years, when buyers appeared, he would show only two or three canvases. "I can't let people roam around here and choose whatever they may have their hearts set on," he commented. "I would be stuck with nothing but the left-overs. I've already sold far too many paintings. Soon I won't be able to work anymore—I've sold pictures I need to have on hand to be able to continue working."

In Munch's last year, there was hardly one picture in ten he felt he could part with. To trade pictures with other artists did not interest him either. The distinguished

Danish painter Jens F. Willumsen, featured in a major exhibit in Oslo, wrote Munch asking him to select one of the paintings on view and send one of his own in return. Munch did not reply. In a new letter, Willumsen asked Munch if he would select *two* pictures from the exhibit in return for one of his own—again no reply.

Apropos letters, it happened that Munch left his mail unopened. If, on a certain day, he received a number of letters he would open only those that gave the appearance of being "pleasant". For this reason, many of his bills remained unsettled, so that, for instance, his electricity might suddenly be turned off.

It was not uncommon that Munch simply gave paintings away—and invariably good ones. To learn later on that such gifts had been sold would disturb him deeply. "Couldn't he have sold something else?" he would ask —"some old clothes, perhaps? Or maybe he could have gone without dinner for a few days, doctors say people eat too much anyway. Personally, I feel much better when I eat moderately. Just imagine, to sell a painting that was a gift from me!"

The European financial crisis which started in the fall of 1920 made it difficult for Munch to maintain his earlier prices. Thus, in the years immediately following the crisis he sold very few paintings. This, in part, was motivated by a desire to protect the investment of those who had already purchased his works. The volume of prints he sold was also considerably reduced. In these years of sharply receding market values, Munch's paintings would bring from five to ten thousand *kroner* and a print from one hundred to three hundred. Having promised the Berlin art dealer Cassirer, who had purchased a large collection of prints, not to sell additional copies of his earliest graphic works, Munch began in the 1930's to color some of the prints he had on hand. Eventually, he produced several hundred such colored prints, all unusually beautiful. He did not often use water colors or colored pencils, a curious fact considering how easily he might have conjured up magic effects by a few brush strokes or touches of pencil color.

Strange at it seems, the prices paid for Munch's prints had nothing to do with the scarcity of the edition. The contrary seemed to be the case. The woodcuts, of which only very few copies existed, reached their maximum in 1939 when a copy of *The Kiss* was sold for five hundred *kroner*. The same subject as an etching sold for six hundred, and an etching of *Sick Girl in a Landscape* brought nine hundred *kroner*. The lithographs, issued in much larger editions than the woodcuts and the etchings, sold in 1939 at prices ranging from one hundred to six hundred *kroner*. At a major sale in Oslo in the 1930's the original drawing for a print brought fifty *kroner* less than the graphic version! Few have collected Munch drawings, while thousands have collected his prints.

Of his lithographs, *Strindberg* and *Self-Portrait with a Skeletal Hand* are the most popular. These brought from six to nine hundred *kroner* in the 1930's. Of greatest monetary value, however, is *Sick Girl* which exists in four editions of one hundred copies each—in red, blue, yellow, and black—and brought the artist four thousand *kroner* in 1920 and again in 1939.

Madonna exists in three separate series of color lithographs with a total edition of more than two hundred fifty prints for which collectors in the 1930's paid an average of twelve hundred *kroner*. The color lithograph *Vampire*, a subject also available in black and white, brought nine hundred *kroner*, while the much rarer woodcuts *Mother and Daughter on the Shore* and *In the Woods* averaged seven hundred *kroner*.

Munch must have produced more than two thousand paintings. The full extent of his work in water color and colored pencils is not as yet known. Of drawings and sketches, however, he did more than five thousand, and his print production reached fifty thousand. Although the total value of all this would stagger the imagination Munch himself reaped only modest financial gains. In his last years, when he could have sold for millions, he refused to let go of more than a few pictures, only as many as was absolutely necessary to provide a limited amount of money for daily needs. Generally, he sold only during the first months of the year, and when three or four pictures had left Ekely he would breathe a sigh of relief and sadness:

"Thank goodness, now I'm through with the sales business for this year. It's terrible that an artist has to sell his works. All I require is enough money to be free to paint in peace and quiet and provide shelter for my pictures. I'm no Vigeland,* you know—I have to sell to exist."

It hurt him to think that anyone might consider him rich.

"Rich," he said; "rich people steal from society, and he who gives alms steals twice as much, for he steals hearts too.... Really, my sales haven't amounted to a great deal," he continued. "At first, my pictures brought so little that is was of no use to sell. Now I get so much for them that I don't need to sell."

And there was a good deal of truth in that paradox. And so, because of his fondness for his own pictures and his great reluctance to part with them, he retained all of his major works and ultimately was able to present the city of Oslo with a collection of unique quality and proportions.

* Reference to the sculptor Gustav Vigeland whose park project was generously supported by the Oslo municipality.

Relationship with Other Artists

Hypersensitive and reserved, Edvard Munch felt drawn only to those whose personality traits resembled his own. His curious friendship with August Strindberg may also explain his strong affinity for literary artists such as Ibsen and Obstfelder and the philosophers Nietzsche and Kierkegaard. The latter occupied him particularly during his last years, although there is no direct reflection of Kierkegaard's thoughts in Munch's paintings.

His relationship with Mrs. Förster-Nietzsche has already been touched upon. As an apropos to one of his favorite quotes from Nietzsche, "When you call on a woman don't forget the whip," he would add with a mischievous gleam: "Nietzsche ought to have used that whip a little on his own sister."

Munch did not as a rule care to illustrate literary works. Ibsen's plays, however, furnished him with much inspiration, and graphic works and paintings often reflect Ibsen subjects: themes from *Peer Gynt, The Pretenders, Ghosts, When We Dead Awaken,* and *Rosmersholm*. The last of these dramas, Munch called "the greatest winter landscape in Norwegian art."

The noted German actor, Alexander Moissi, said that Munch's print *Oswald* inspired him deeply in his attempt to interpret this character in *Ghosts*. Elevated by Munch's portrayal of Oswald, broken and paralyzed, bringing his mother to the point of collapse by declaring that he is hopelessly diseased, Moissi developed this particular scene into the dramatic climax of the play.

I have heard Munch say that he extracted much picture

material from Obstfelder's poetry. *The Shriek* may well have been an interpretation of the anguished conclusion reached by the poet in *I Look:*

I look at the well-dressed men,
I look at the smiling ladies,
I look at the straining horses ...

How heavy are the blue gray clouds!

I look, I look ...
I have surely come upon a wrong planet,
It is so strange here. . . .

Introverts like Munch have no love for boisterous individuals, dandelions who tend to choke the more sensitive flowers. Thus, Norway's popular leader in the second half of the nineteenth century, Bjørnstjerne Bjørnson—poet, novelist, dramatist, winner of the Nobel Prize for Literature, everactive and opinionated—was a thorn in Munch's eyes.

"Look at Bjørnson," he scoffed. "Big, broad, robust like a pope. Anyone wanting to shake my hand line up over here. You know, he actually lived long enough to write something stupid about me. Ugh, how robust he was"—Munch shuddered—"oozing horse and peasant romance!"

Munch, always willing to help struggling artists financially, actually care little for contemporary art, rarely visited exhibits, and never purchased a drawing or a painting by another artist. Instead, he bought cheap reproductions of art works—mostly Rembrandt but occasionally some of his own contemporaries—tacked them up on his walls and left them there until they fell down of their own accord. He also bought a few art books and magazines which he leafed through now and then—that, he felt, was exposure enough.

The three major artists from whom he seems to have

learned the most are Toulouse-Lautrec, Van Gogh, and Gauguin. Despite the great technical similarity between the works of Munch and those of Toulouse-Lautrec, Munch apparently never bought a reproduction of a Toulouse-Latrec painting, nor did he talk much about him—or of Gauguin, for that matter. Van Gogh, on the other hand, truly fascinated him. He told me once, as a curiosity, that this first exposure to a painting by Van Gogh left no impression on him at all.

"At least, I can't remember that it did," he said. "But now, of all the paintings in our National Gallery the small canvas by Van Gogh is the one that intrigues me the most—it frightens me, almost. I have often stood in the door opening of the room where it hangs and observed the picture carefully. If I walk up close to it I see some red spots that irritate me—it seems that someone has scratched the canvas ... or perhaps the picture is a sketch Van Gogh has started and someone else finished? Like that Karsten painting you bought, the one of the coffin with the family pictures on the wall in the background. That must be a half-finished picture I gave Karsten once when he needed a canvas. The floor and the walls are his, but the rest is just as I left it. Perhaps that's why he didn't sign it. Karsten did this sort of thing often, I've heard. In Paris he used to buy pictures by other painters and keep working on them—Christian Krohg did too. When poor friends needed money Krohg would give their paintings a few touches and add his signature to make the pictures worth fifty or a hundred *kroner*. I myself painted a little on one of Krohg's pictures—that large *Albertine* canvas in the National Gallery. Otherwise I've stayed away from such activities.

"Kittelsen, the fairytale champion," he went on, "asked me once if we might try to make a picture together, a big troll parading up Karl Johan Street. Kittelsen would do the troll and I the rest. Nothing came of it.... You know, I liked Kittelsen—a screwball really, became infuriated when others tried to paint his beloved trolls and goblins. 'What business does that fellow have painting my trolls and goblins,' he would say. 'That damned idiot has never seen any of those creatures!'"

Munch's early mentors, Christian Krohg and Erik Werenskiold, were never his favorites. The thoroughly healthy and robust air that seemed to exude from them repelled him, made him apprehensive, and caused conflicts which left indelible scars.

Most of the other leading Norwegian artists of the period immediately preceding his own, Frits Thaulow, Eilif Peterssen, Hans Heyerdahl, and Gerhard Munthe he also stayed away from, although for one of them, Heyerdahl, he had words of praise:

"It's not right of Jens Thiis to insist that I have learned so much from Christian Krohg. From Heyerdahl, however, I have learned something. As a human being he was among the worst, I think ... he and Eilif Peterssen," he added, "but there is something very sound in Heyerdahl's early pictures."

Among Norwegian painters slightly younger than himself his favorite remained Ludvig Karsten with whom he even spent an entire summer in Aasgaardstrand—during the more sociable period of his early years. Especially after Karsten's death Munch talked about him frequently. Karsten, often aloof and arrogant toward others, idolized Munch and his art. If Munch happened to enter a room Karsten would rise and greet him as he might have greeted the Lord himself.

"Munch is the only one who amounts to anything," he would say. "The others can neither paint nor draw. They're using shoe polish and call it 'the deep organ tone in Norwegian painting'—hypocrites pretending to be profound thinkers. Munch is the only one who masters the technique of drawing too. Look at the rest—posing their models stiffly. Munch now—he makes them crouch up into infernal, shrunken beasts. Whatever the other paint the result is nothing but artifical poses. Although they paint and paint with great industry, they're still so dead and empty-headed that they see nothing beyond what an ordinary human being sees."

Karsten, son of a well-to-do businessman, kept borrowing clothes and canvases from his friends and only rarely returned any of these items. When Karsten's father died one of these friends approached the painter and said: "I understand you have a lot of money now?"

"Who says so?"

"The papers do. I saw it when they published the income tax returns," his friend replied. "And in view of your elevated status you ought not parade around in *my* pants."

"Take care," Karsten warned. "Remember you're talking to a man of means!"

Jens Thiis, Munch's faithful admirer, fared no better than Krohg and Werenskiold in his relationship with the sensitive artist. Thiis's first transgression was to be seen in the company of artists Munch disliked. Then, when Munch heard Thiis speak favorably of paintings he himself did not appreciate, he retaliated by painting a very unflattering portrait of Thiis in which the director of the National Gallery is pictured as a broad, bulky figure in yellow and green.

Munch's sensitivity might even express itself in direct violence. In his early years, he once attended a special artists' celebration. The master of ceremonies, a painter who had repeatedly expressed open disapproval of Munch's works, now believing Munch had come to the party uninvited, approached him and said: "You don't belong here. This is a party for artists."

A few years later, Munch happened to meet the same person in Aasgaardstrand and promptly pulled a gun on him after which he forced him to pose for a painting. "Really, all I wanted to do," Munch said gleefully in recalling the episode, "was to portray a truly frightened man."

Munch's relationship with the younger generation was no better than with the older. He never encouraged young painters to call on him. His circle of friends was very limited, and there were no artists in it. Included were Jappe Nielsen, the critic, Sigurd Høst, philologist and art connoisseur, the opera singer Halfdan Rode, and Kristian Schreiner, a well-known physician. During the last two years of his life, Munch invited Dr. Schreiner to Ekely quite regularly and even asked him to look over some notes he had written.

On rare occasions, Munch would allow foreign artists and critics to call on him. Until 1939 he was particularly cordial to such visitors from Germany, even art dealers. "After all," he would say, "The Germans have done a great deal for me."

Only one of Norway's younger artists was a frequent visitor at Ekely, Pola Gauguin, son of the French master. Munch liked Gauguin's work as art critic in *Dagbladet*, his favorite newspaper; and of the two major Norwegian Munch biographies written during the artist's lifetime, one by Jens Thiis and the other by Pola Gauguin, Munch much preferred the latter.

"Gauguin's book is written by a painter, that fact shines through on every page. Most of the material Jens Thiis presents I seem to have read somewhere else."

He lamented only one aspect of Gauguin's book: the relatively superficial treatment of the artist's relationship with women. "If it's necessary to write a book about me," he said with a touch of pride, "it shouldn't be such a *proper* book. I'm no old maid, you know."

It is interesting to note that Munch steadfastly refused to talk to either Jens Thiis or Pola Gauguin while they were writing their books about him.

I said that Munch never purchased paintings by other artists. That's not entirely true. Once, he confided to me, he bought a canvas by a painter whom he later suspected of plotting against him. The artist, having helped Munch hang pictures for an exhibit, followed shortly with an exhibit of his own, and Munch purchased a painting for one thousand *kroner*.

"I bought it," he said, "because it was the only one that was not already sold."

Munch never attended meetings of the Artists Association, and he stubbornly refused to take part in group exhibits. After repeated requests, the jury selecting work for the annual state exhibit received his permission to come out to Ekely to choose a few canvases.

"Take whatever you like," Munch told them affably.

"What about this?" one of the jury members suggested.

"No, that one you can't take—I must keep that here." And the same reaction followed each of their selections. Finally, the jury had to leave with only one small sketch.

When my own collection was to be shown he asked anxiously: "I'll get a separate room for my paintings, won't I?"

The day before the opening he came down to preview the exhibit and found two pictures by another artist displayed with his own. He promptly took a taxi back to Ekely and returned shortly with two large canvases. "Please, hang these in place of those other two—these are from *The Frieze of Life*, you know."

Two groups dominated the art scene in the Norwegian capital from 1915 to 1935, the so-called "warm red" group and the "cold blue." The "warm red," the larger of the two, centered around Henrik Sørensen, perhaps next to Edvard Munch the most influential painter in Norwegian history. To this group belonged Per Krohg, Axel Revold, and Alf Rolfsen, the "mural brothers," as Munch preferred to call them, and Reidar Aulie, Willi Midelfart, Joronn Sitje, Hugo Lous Mohr, and many others who had found in Henrik Sørensen a tireless friend and spokesman. A deep concern for spiritual and social problems their trademark, they tend to deny the importance of the "blue" decorative art of painters like Ludvig Karsten. Paradoxically, perhaps, they respond favorably to works by Matisse and their own countryman Thorvald Erichsen, both undeniably "blue". The members of this group, as well as all other Norwegian painters who became established in the years between the two wars, viewed Munch with admiration and respect. Nevertheless, they have little in common with him. In a way, they all reflect a healthier outlook and are, therefore, far more common. Edvard Munch, the recluse, was not their ideal. They —especially Henrik Sørensen—would have preferred to mold Munch into a pillar of society.

There was in Henrik Sørensen a primeval strength. Intelligent and dynamic, he had a host of friends and wielded considerable power. He assisted hundreds of young artists, provided buyers for their works and stipends from the government. Calling Munch "The Great Master" he still found it difficult to accept his senior's aloofness. As human beings Sørensen and Munch were stark contrasts. Sørensen, never too busy to be involved, seemingly omnipresent and inexhaustible, always on the go, spreading influence wherever he established contact—like a living newspaper. A true friend of the Jews he still painted Christ as a blond Nordic god. Only Edvard Munch and one other important artist remained untouched by Henrik Sørensen's efforts.

"No, I don't believe in this Nordic Jesus," Munch said, referring to Henrik Sørensen. "I'm sure he means well and occasionally says something worthwhile. The trouble is that he talks incessantly. I really don't understand how he finds time to paint.

"He calls me up and tells me to get out of bed earlier in the morning; that I must send money and pictures here and there—as if I'm expected to provide for the entire southern half of our country.

"I know why he likes to run around like that, though," he whispered in confidence. "He had kidney stones. One day he actually pulled out a small box and showed me a kidney stone." Munch shook his head in exasperation. "Did you ever see a worse dandelion? I tell you, that man is really spreading his seeds around."

The personality contrast between the two is clearly reflected in their individual color choices. Munch loved bright sunny hues in preference to the nocturnal light of the moon. Henrik Sørensen's pictures, on the other hand, sometimes give the appearance of having been painted with moonlight in the brush. His favorite colors are an impetuous red, a phosphorescent, mosslike gray, and pale shades of yellow and blue; and he does not shy away from the use of brown.

Munch always spoke very favorably about Per Krohg, one of the "mural brothers" who was his godchild. He liked his drawings and felt that Per Krohg was a greater artist than his father, Christian Krohg.

The other artist who remained outside of Henrik Sørensen's sphere of influence was Henrik Lund, spokesman for the "cold blue" group. He and his followers shared the other group's admiration for Munch. However, concerned only with the creation of beautiful pictures and totally indifferent to social problems, they also admired Ludvig Karsten. Among them were Bernhard Folkestad, Per Deberitz, Astri Welhaven Heiberg, Arne Kavli, Bernt Clüver, and Torstein Torsteinson.

Munch was equally scathing in his scorn for this group, however, and he saw in Henrik Lund an intelligent, sociable, and skilled artist who compensated for his lack of depth by applying to his work a sophisticated taste and great technical finesse. It was as easy for him as for Henrik Sørensen to establish important contacts and provide buyers for his own and his friends' pictures.

One day Munch happened to visit an exhibit of Henrik Lund's works. Learning of this by telephone, Henrik Lund rushed by car to the gallery, reached it after closing time and found Munch alone.

"Well, what do you think?" he asked apprehensively.

Munch did not answer.

"Please, Edvard, tell me what you think!"

Munch looked at him. "You're clever," he said. "It's remarkable what you have been able to do—without having a true spark."

"Don't I have a spark?"

"No, you don't, but you have taste. You learn a bit here and a bit there and combine it all refreshingly and with great flourish."

"Don't I have a spark?" Lund persisted.

Munch looked at him again, very penetratingly, and said:

"Tell me, Henrik, don't you have an inner life at all?"

But Munch was not entirely negative in his judgment of Henrik Lund's position in Norwegian art. "I'm glad we have Henrik Lund," he said. "He stands as a practical countermeasure against all these peasants. We have too much Nordic Christ, poorhouses, and Telemark," he continued, thinking mainly of Henrik Sørensen and the rural part of Norway which figures so prominently in Sørensen's art. "I'm against all sorts of cliques. Artists must develop their own individual marks—must work alone. But as long as we do have cliques anyway, I'd rather see many than only one."

In the 1920's Munch asked me if I had any idea what Vigeland was doing. At that time I lived in a house right next to Vigeland's "palace", and it happened that I crawled up on the fence between our properties to look at the sculpture groups Vigeland had standing outside. I told Munch what I had seen, and he asked if I might be able to take a few pictures of the groups. I enlisted the aid of one of Vigeland's stone cutters—he had thirteen! However, before we were able to snap any pictures Vigeland caught me sitting on the fence. I had never seen him before and became frightened when he was suddenly standing there before me like a giant whom God had decided to pound one foot shorter. His head seemed to protrude from a cavity in his shoulders, and his width and height appeared about equal. When I think of it now there was something in his facial expression and build which reminds me of Mussolini. Rumor had it that he could become so enraged that he would chase people with crowbars and chisels. When this happened his stone cutters would scramble over the fence and head across the fields as fast as their feet would carry them. Knowing this, I instinctively jumped off the fence and ran.

The following day I wrote him a letter of apology and

promised never to scale the fence again. In reply, one of Vigeland's friends called me on behalf of the sculptor to express his appreciation for the letter and invite me to see Vigeland's works the following Sunday when the master himself would act as guide. I might bring a friend too.

This development I reported to Munch and asked him to join me.

The thought obviously intrigued him. "I haven't seen Vigeland since that time in Berlin," he said. "It might be very interesting...."

I wrote Vigeland and said that Edvard Munch might possibly accompany me if that would be acceptable. When I drove out to Munch to pick him up that Sunday, however, he was not there. His housekeeper told me he had left. And, when I arrived at Vigeland's "palace", I was shown around by the sculptor's friend. Vigeland, too, had backed out.

Many years later, I accompanied a group of Danish artists to Vigeland's workshop. The gatekeeper stopped me, called Vigeland on the phone and asked if I might enter. The answer was negative. A couple of other Norwegians in the party were let in with the Danes.

One day, on receipt of his annual notice from the Internal Revenue Department, Munch really fumed:

"When I think of how they keep treating me in this country I feel like tearing up my last will and testament. And do you know what I would put in it instead of what's there now? I'd say: 'To the Norwegian people I give the sculptor Gustav Vigeland—column, sun dial, and fountain.'"

For a while, Munch was quite impressed with the works of the young Norwegian Aage Storstein. After I had shown him one of the Storstein paintings in my collection he asked me to come out to Ekely the next day. On arrival, I found that he had placed his own favorite paintings in a continuous row from the gate to the house.

"Storstein must have seen quite a bit of Picasso," he

said. "His colors are beautiful, and the cubes are all right." Walking up and down in front of his own works, he continued: "There's too much moss and twigs here. But I don't suppose it will be long before we tire of these cubes too. Even so, it's fine to have some cubes and triangles; it develops discipline, shows us the close relationship that exists between art and mathematics. There's latent mathematics in all forms of art. Cubes tend to offset the fanciful and excessively sweet."

Munch painted portraits of many of his contemporaries —scientists, poets, and composers, but rarely painters and never actors or actresses. He formed no bonds of friendship with great men of his day. One of the reasons may have been that he found it very difficult to praise anyone. Although he knew that praise would be paid in kind he refused to flatter.

From 1915 and on, Munch's position as Norway's—and one of the world's—foremost painters was indisputable. Nevertheless, he remained stubbornly suspicious even toward those who praised him most generously. Only twice did he publicly speak up on behalf of a Norwegian painter; the first time when Henrik Sørensen wanted all of Ludvig Karsten's pictures removed from the National Gallery.

"That wall with Karsten's pictures is the best thing they have down there," he declared. "I know perfectly well that if Karsten's works are removed, mine will be next on the list. Please, quote me on that to those who have anything to do with these matters. You know some people of the press, don't you? By the way, this ought to be a good time to buy Karsten paintings. I'm sure there are few who dare do it."

Munch's defense of Karsten spread quickly in art circles, and the campaign against the pictures soon ceased. Of course, Jens Thiis, the director, was particularly fond of Karsten's works and had personally gathered all the pictures for the magnificent Karsten wall.

The second time Munch publicly praised a fellow artist

was when the young, and then almost totally unknown, Erik Harry Johannessen suffered a nervous breakdown.

"This man is really good," he commented as he looked at Johannessen's paintings. "He knows how to work with black, that's something I have never been able to do. He is sick, you say? That does not surprise me. He must have suffered a great deal. These pictures reflect tremendous spiritual stress. Why don't you send him a thousand *kroner* from me and tell him that his pictures have moved me deeply."

Johannessen did not accept the money. He had become a religious fanatic and was waiting for the second coming of Christ. "Thousands who are now living will never die," he stated. "Instead, they will be taken directly up to the Lord. It's in the Scriptures."

Sad to say, Scriptures also stated that thou shalt not make idols. Therefore Erik Harry Johannessen refused to paint and to accept money earned in sin. "Christ will provide money," he said, "from day to day."

His last great canvas, an altar painting presenting Christ as a bride, he burned. Instead of painting he turned to the more prosaic occupation of decorating store windows.

Since flattery was abhorrent to Munch and he never really cared particularly what happened to his fellow artists, his praise of Ludvig Karsten and Erik Harry Johannessen must have been motivated by a feeling of close affinity with these two, a conviction that they were, somehow, of *his* emotional fiber.

Ekely

The main building of Ekely, yellow in color, is an ugly structure from the 1890's, two stories high with a central dormer. Munch lived on the first floor. The second, as well as basement and attic, served as storage area and contained paintings and piles of drawings and prints. No one was allowed on these particular premises.

"No, no, don't come up here," he warned me. "I'll find that etching myself. Stay there; I don't want anyone up here. All you'll find are a few little children asleep.

"Look at that," he said with obvious pride as he came down half an hour later with a woodcut in his hand. "I really hit on something there, didn't I? Cubes long before Picasso." He scanned the picture carefully. "When could I have done it, I wonder? Oh yes, now I remember. Maybe I'll get back to cubes again sometime—but then, everyone would say I was just trying to imitate Picasso."

On the first floor were kitchen, bath, and four other rooms. When Munch had a housekeeper the kitchen, at least, was kept neat.

Except for a grand piano, his furnishings were Spartan and consisted of a bed, an upholstered bench, a grandfather clock, a mirror, a few family portraits he had inherited, and three tables and nine chairs, among these the black wicker chair featured in *Sick Girl*.

Dishes and flatware were neat but simple—just five cups, eight glasses, and six place settings of knives, forks, and spoons.

His lamps were without shades, his windows without curtains, and the floors bare. He did buy a few very fine rugs at one time but removed them very quickly. They seemed so useless, he thought.

For thirty years Munch lived at Ekely. When he died the house was almost as empty as when he moved in.

The grand piano he had acquired in exchange for a picture. Now and then he'd sit down and play it, he said, but I know of no one who ever heard Munch play, nor did he to my knowledge ever ask anyone else to play. He did, however, have a big radio which was left on day and night. His lamps were always lit too—Munch was afraid of the dark.

Once, when he asked me to come out to Ekely in the evening, I brought a friend along and forgot to ask Munch's permission to do so. The result was that I alone was let in while my friend was forced to wait at the gate. After a while I pleaded for him:

"Couldn't you possibly let my friend come in? It's so dark outside."

"Dark? Oh yes, so it is. Pardon me, I didn't think of the dark."

My friend entered, but, since Munch refused to talk to him, left again shortly.

"Was he a painter?" Munch inquired. "Why did you bring him out here, anyway? You know perfectly well I can't talk to more than one person at the time. I'm very busy with something right now"—his agitation increased—"and I can't allow another human being to enter my mind. And when I meet a person I can't help asking myself, 'What kind of fellow is he? What does he think of my pictures?' And I can't settle down until I have painted him. Don't you see what that means? I can't paint anything new right now. I've got to finish the picture I'm working on, Kollmann as Faust."

It was not for the sake of economy that Munch refrained from buying furniture. He simply did not care to have his house attractive or comfortable—didn't even buy himself a good chair. When it came to providing space for his pictures, however, he was quite a spendthrift and erected three separate buildings at Ekely, the last of these, a brick structure, designed by himself.

At first, he invited a contractor to submit complete

plans of the building, but none of these met with his approval. Karsten, meeting Munch one day, asked: "How are the plans coming for that new building you're going to put up?"

"The building?" Munch scoffed in disgust. "It has cost me twelve hundred *kroner* just to talk about it."

So he proceeded with his own plans and construction got under way. It turned out to be a tall, narrow building, resembling, perhaps, a cross between a power plant and a white coffin.

And there were the sheds he built to protect his paintings—a six-foot-wide overhang above a tall fence, the floor simply an extension of his lawn. Everywhere—in the new building, along the walls of the sheds, in the house— were hundreds and hundreds of canvases. Often, searching in vain in all this space for a specific painting, he would finally be sure it had been stolen and call me up in frustration:

"This is Munch," he would announce abruptly. "Something is wrong out here. One of my best paintings has been stolen, an important canvas in *The Frieze of Life,* the one with the wave that washes in over the beach. Do you remember it? It's about three feet square—or perhaps rather a bit oblong—" his description was vague—"green, blue, and green. Aha, so you do remember it. But do you happen to remember where I keep it? Couldn't you come up here and help me look for it? I need it for something I'm working on right now."

On tables and chairs and on the floor were brushes, canvases, and tubes; on the grand piano a pile of letters and prints; and in the attic and the basement were prints, hand presses, copper plates, and print stones. The house was really one big mess. He always needed a couple of days to prepare for visitors, and, when going through such preparations, would pace up and down, straightening out a little, swearing loudly, and declare his disgust at the waste of time involved in social activities.

"It's only when you keep cleaning and dusting that dirt is bothersome. If you just leave it alone it stays in its place."

Ekely was surrounded by a high barbed-wire fence, and the gates had built-in locks as well as padlocks. He kept big, vicious dogs around—so vicious that he didn't dare pet them himself. Dogs become wicked when chained, and Munch's dogs were chained with steel.

"Easy now," he would say apprehensively as he approached the barking dogs. "Can't you see it's just your lord and master who's coming? Haven't I given you a brother to play with and a roof over your head? And so much food that you're ready to burst?"

Munch, no animal lover, did paint some very good animal pictures, mostly horses and dogs. After several visits to a circus, he prepared a folder of drawings of wild animals, all excellent. Many consist only of a few lines—all the same, they sparkle with life and energy.

It is no cliche to say that Edvard Munch did not care about money, that all he craved was to be able to paint undisturbed. He worked, ate, and slept in the same room. To have people around, even a housekeeper, plagued and irritated him.

"They all try to gain power over me," he complained. "They make me eat when food is ready whether I'm hungry or not. They slow me down, bother me with trivial questions while I work—'shouldn't I buy crackers? Do you want a steak?'"

Munch insisted that visitors telephone before calling on him in person. Then, if for some reason or other he wouldn't feel up to it he would say so. As he approached old age his desire to see people diminished radically. The higher the prospective visitor ranked on the social or cultural ladder the more diligently Munch felt he had to pay attention to the condition of the house; consequently all pleasure vanished.

Of course, he did not like to call on others either and was particularly apprehensive about parties. This aversion for social gatherings may be traced all the way back to his reaction to the atmosphere in Jacobsen's psychiatric clinic.

"I feel like a prisoner when I attend parties," he said, "and I don't want to be anyone's prisoner—my nerves can't take it. To sit for hours at the table, I mean, and wait for others to finish, and then be forced into politeness, watch myself so I don't say the wrong thing. Really, it gets on my nerves. I can't take it. Nor can I stand to listen to conversations about subjects I know nothing about.

"I don't drink anything either, and I have to stay away from strong foods. That really upsets a host, you know.

"'What can we offer you, Mr. Munch?' they ask. 'There must be something you can drink, isn't there?'

"I have quit eating meat too now—it makes me nauseated to see someone slice into a roast and see the blood trickle. Actually, I don't like to see people eat."

When on rare occasions Munch actually did attend a party he would usually arrive quite early and make this announcement to his host:

"I've kept my taxi waiting—I'll have to leave in a minute."

And if he caught sight of someone he did not like, or did not know, he would take his leave immediately. If not, he might stay for a considerable time, especially if his own pictures were on the walls.

"They're hanging very nicely here," he would say, "although I used to think my pictures needed large exhibit halls—great distances. It isn't easy to comprehend the totality of a picture at a distance of only ten feet. You know, I don't care to paint fingernails and such details; I'd rather have people see the *totality*"—he lingered on the word—"my pictures may well hang a little in the dark—that makes it easier to see the totality."

In the right mood, Munch would gladly talk about his pictures, about his life, and about people and events. He used few gestures when he talked—the most typical and frequent was his tendency to wave his arms when he talked about problems beyond his control. He would lift his arms, flap them like wings, then drop them limply down to his thighs in a convincing gesture of helplessness.

His sentences came in short, broken fragments, but steadily, like water rushing over stony rapids. He was not to be stopped. This uninterrupted verbal flow was obviously a protective measure. He wanted to avoid being asked questions, and even when he himself asked he often went right on without waiting for an answer. He seemed able to read the reply in the other person's face. One topic followed the other without seeming coherence:

"That Hitler, now, he must be crazy, don't you think? To let loose a war like this one. I understand he doesn't like my pictures. Of course, those who have painted up and down with broad brushes can't stand us who paint with the art size. I'm too old to keep up with the happenings down there. They'll have to do whatever the devil dictates, I guess. I can't be bothered with it. They've even sold a painting of mine that was donated by someone or other to the Dresden Gallery." He waved his arms and let them fall again.

"He may conquer England, but he'll never beat America. I have faith in the Russians too—they've always been great warriors. He's gone in for city planning now, I understand. All of Berlin is going to be one big Victory Boulevard. He'll be busy. It's much better to paint with smaller brushes, if you're asking me. I think you ought to let those two pictures change places. The winter landscape doesn't need that much light. You should have bought that picture from Dresden, remember? What about Goebbels? Do you think he's just as crazy? He sent me a letter on my seventieth birthday—'I greet you as the greatest painter of the Germanic world,' he said. I wonder what has happened to him—perhaps he has been fired. He owned a couple of my etchings. You really should have bought that picture from Dresden."

Sometimes he locked himself into his rooms at Ekely, and days would pass when no words were exchanged between him and his housekeeper. When he wanted something to eat he would unlock the door and enter the kitchen, and when he had finished eating he would lock himself in again. The housekeeper might enter the kitchen while he was there.

"Is Mr. Munch angry with me?" she would ask.

"Haven't I told you I must have absolute quiet?" he would snap. "Don't you have a friend or a relative you can invite out here and talk to? I have no objection. You can take as much fruit in the garden as you wish. I've told you that many times. I pay good wages too. I've got to have it quiet around here."

If he fired his housekeeper the reason was always the same: "She didn't leave me alone—was always knocking on doors, always asking about something."

He tried several times to get along without domestic help. He would prepare his own food and even scrub floors. His cooking was very simple—for dinner mostly bread and soup, or water, some vegetables, and a piece of fish. Not wanting to clean the fish, he would cut off the tail and cook that instead of the main part. If he couldn't lay his hands on a lid he might cover the pan with a print—once it was *Sick Girl*.

"Watch out!" someone standing by shouted. "Don't you realize it is *Sick Girl* you're using?"

"So what?" he replied calmly. "It doesn't cost me anything. In fact, it'll be interesting to see it steamed."

It was true that Munch paid good wages to those who kept house for him. Though they had little to do and much free time it was still not easy for him to keep a capable housekeeper. The loneliness at Ekely was oppressive, and it was difficult to adjust to his peculiar ways. His housekeepers thought it curious, for instance, that he would let the fruit rot on the trees; and they found it nerve-racking to have the lights burning and the radio blaring at all hours. As for the radio, it was not music or news that interested him. He wanted to hear voices—any kind of voices no matter what they said or what language they said it in. He craved a continuous and quite loud sound of voices and didn't always bother to tune in the radio carefully.

"Last Sunday morning," he told me, "I amused myself by listening to two preachers speak at the same time. None of them wanted to give in. Do you comprehend what preachers are saying? Death, where is thy sting, and hell, where is thy victory? Halleluia and amen! It's strange with all these sounds and voices that fill the air. I think of it often—can't dismiss the thought from my mind by telling myself, 'it's only sound waves.'"

Months had passed without Munch having a house-keeper.

"Perhaps I'd better get myself a housekeeper again," he suggested. "Although it certainly gives you a fine feeling to be your own master. Kaiser Wilhelm amused himself by sawing wood. It might be just as amusing to scrub floors. This summer I have actually *painted* floors too.

"It's marvelous not to be surrounded by these eternal questions of 'What does Mr. Munch want for dinner today?' and 'Would you want some cheese?'

"All right,' I say, patient as an angel, 'why don't you buy some cheese? I'm tired of rusks and crackers. Isn't there something else? All I need is a simple prison diet.'

"'What does Mr. Munch mean by that?' she asks ominously.

"So I have to put down my brushes for the thousandth time and explain: 'I can't eat fatty foods. Buy whatever you want—rusks and crackers, as far as I am concerned. Could I possibly be allowed to paint a little now?'

"A couple of days later she is back:

"'What about the fruit in the orchard, Mr. Munch? Shouldn't we pick it—buy crates, sell it at the market?'

"'Do exactly as you want,' I say. 'Just don't bother me with it. I don't want to pick fruit and bring it to the market. I'm trying to paint a little—that's all I'm trying to do.'

"But she is not satisfied, of course. 'I received no reply from Mr. Munch regarding the apples,' she says. 'And now Mr. Svendsen, the caretaker, has asked me to inquire whether we ought not have the horse shod.'

"Can you beat that? Well, 'Eat as many apples as you want,' I say. 'Don't you have some friends? Ask them to come with their baskets and pick as much as they like. The rest will fall by itself. I don't have time for market sales. As for Svendsen, he can arrange for the horse-shoeing by himself. Am I supposed to be a stable boy too? Tell Svendsen he can sell the horse for all I care. I've painted it so often there's nothing left in it!'

"A few minutes pass and she knocks on the door again: 'Svendsen says there's something wrong with the horse's legs. We won't get much for it. What price does Mr. Munch have in mind? Svendsen says he knows someone who might give four hundred *kroner* for it.'"

My telephone rang.

"This is Munch. Take a cab and come out as quickly as you can," he urged excitedly. "We've had the damned-est business out here. Do come right away. It's very important—I'm sure we'll have a law suit on our hands. You may have to testify under oath."

When I arrived Munch was pacing the floor. He looked intently at me, waving his arms, and said:

"I'm not going to put words in your mouth. Come and see for yourself. You should have no trouble testifying under oath."

My mind was blank.

"All right, we can go upstairs too. Don't you notice anything?" He grabbed hold of a chair and moved it deliberately to the left and the right.

"Is it the fact that the Florentine leather chairs are gone?"

"That's it," he exclaimed triumphantly. "Didn't I get two Florentine leather chairs from my aunt Sofie's estate? Well, I asked the housekeeper as calmly as I could: 'Where are the Florentine leather chairs?' I asked. I must be allowed to ask about my own chairs, don't you think? Well, it has been the damnedest life here ever since. Weeping and moaning all over the place.

"'Do you think I'm stealing?' she asks.

"'I must be allowed to ask about my own chairs,' I reply.

"'There have never been any Florentine chairs in this house,' she sniffles.

"'Didn't I inherit two Florentine chairs from my aunt Sofie? Are you trying to tell me I'm imagining things? Perhaps you think I've never had any Florentine chairs?'

"Well, I got her out of the house and had no sooner sat down than Svendsen comes right in here and says:

"'As long as I have been at Ekely there have been no Florentine leather chairs in the house.' That's what he had the nerve to tell me right to my face. So I got him out too. Finally, the housekeeper's aunt marches in:

"'There has never been a thief in my family,' she declares. 'And I've told Petra that she will receive free legal assistance. Svendsen has promised to testify.'

"'I must be allowed to inquire about my own chairs,' I persist. 'Is there going to be a lawsuit about this thing?'" His arms dropped limply to his side, and he looked at me.

"I did not put words in your mouth, remember that. Remember, it was you who said, 'Is it the fact that the Florentine leather chairs are gone?'"

"That's right," I said. "I can certainly swear that there used to be two Florentine leather chairs in this room."

"Of course. Of course there have been Florentine leather chairs in the room. I inherited them from aunt Sofie. But I don't give a damn about the chairs!"

Later, the entire problem was solved when it turned out that Munch a few months earlier had sent the chairs to his sister Inger.

The ‹Golden› Years

The most prosperous period in Edvard Munch's life was undoubtedly the interval between 1913 and 1930. Very few artists have experienced a similar surge of popularity and fame. All Scandinavian galleries and hundreds of private collectors, big and small, vied for his pictures. Had he wanted to sell his own collection he would have become one of Norway's richest men. A threatening mental crisis lay safely in the past, and his physical condition was excellent. Nevertheless, convinced that it was his destiny to continue battling forces stronger than himself, he was not happy. "Some are born to be victors," he said, "but I'm not among them."

His success came too late to erase the bleak memories of the past. The anguish of his childhood, in particular, had left such deep scars in his personality that he was incapable of enjoying true happiness. Although he liked to jest and tell stories and really had a great sense of humor he was never able to laugh at his own difficulties.

Completely incorruptible and always trustworthy, he still liked to poke fun at people and spin long, fantastic tales. Stinging at times, he was never vulgar or obscene. He had great ability to formulate sentences that sparkled with dry, biting humor—sentences that came like quick, uninterrupted blows. Had he said something particularly pointed a mischievous expression would flicker across his face—a brief smile. He could laugh too, a loud reverberating laughter. Moments later, however, he would be sad and depressed—a more familiar mood. Constantly afraid his strength would give out, he still kept hoping to get another major work under way, a new frieze.

Most of his toil and struggle, he felt, had been in vain; he had never really succeeded in making his pictures the way *he* wanted them to be. That collectors and connoisseurs praised paintings with which he was dissatisfied gave him no comfort. Often in great doubt as to how he might "correct" a picture, he used to paint separate little patches and attach them to the main canvas with thumbtacks, tear them off again, paint new ones, tear them off—painting and patching until all of a sudden he felt he had arrived.

"Look at that!" he would exclaim jubilantly. "And by sheer accident too. What a lucky break! That's exactly the way I wanted it to be."

Edvard Munch, the artist, was really much more a child of fortune than he himself realized. Few painters have succeeded "by accident" as often as he did. Once under way, he would usually finish a painting in short time. His brushes would whizz across the canvas, glide in long arches. The mixing of colors went quickly too; only the process of finding the right tubes seemed time consuming. Even when painting under apparently deep inspiration, however, he might occasionally get completely stymied.

Munch had few pleasures and most often found life monotonous.

"I keep painting," he said with a shrug of the shoulders; "that's the least monotonous activity I know. I hate to have to do the same things over and over again—get dressed, eat, take the same walks. Every day we've got to do the same things we have done a thousand times before —ten thousand times! Take shaving, for instance. Is there anything more monotonous?"

He often suffered from lack of energy and had to muster great willpower to get started. In the very process of painting much was a burden to him.

"The most disagreeable thing I know is to hunt for brushes and tubes and to lay out colors, but the most difficult problem is to *see*. We paint what we *think* we see. If nanny has said that the cheeks are white and red we paint the cheeks white and red. Actually, they are gray and green. The Greeks painted the sky black—didn't know the color blue. Green is a color no one seemed to know much about until a hundred years ago. Rembrandt's foliage used to be brown. Down in Aasgaardstrand one summer—that year Karsten was with me—I was painting some white cherry blossoms and found that a light effect from the grass made me paint them green. Some curious vacationers pointed this out to me. 'But Mr. Munch,' they said. 'Is that supposed to be cherry blossoms?'

"Soon thereafter Karsten came on the scene. 'Why are you painting the blossoms green?' he asked.

"'They are green.'

"'No, they're red.'

"'Are they red?' I looked at Karsten and then at the blossoms, and by Jove, he was right! The cherry blossoms were red. They must have caught a light reflection from a red cloud.

"Karsten was very sharp, noticed such things right away. Strange, isn't it? I was quite fond of Karsten, actually. Even so ... well, you remember my aiming at him and firing. What would a judge have said if it had come to testifying. 'Your honour, I was really very fond of Karsten.'"

Edvard Munch always felt that someone or something kept him away from his work. The electric bill, for instance, was a constant source of irritation. Since he never opened "unpleasant looking" envelopes, including those from the power company, his electricity was frequently turned off. Then he would have to take time off from his work and go down town to settle the bill. There were always bills to be settled.

"When am I going to find time to paint?" he complained. "It's more as if I'm running a country store—pictures to be sold and goods to be picked up. And this tax problem has made a bookkeeper of me too. I'm really not supposed to paint, I guess. Instead, I'm supposed to sit here and scribble figures in a book. If the figures don't seem to balance I'll be put in prison. Look at Vigeland —they let him use millions! I don't care about money, really. All I want to do is to use the limited time I have left to paint a few pictures in peace and quiet. By now, I have learned a good deal about painting and ought to be able to contribute my best. The country might benefit by giving me time to paint. But does anyone care? I've got to rush down town to pay bills, then rush back home to keep books. Vigeland gets millions—never exhibits, never lets the critics see his work. And now this column he is making, it's my picture *Toward the Light* he has taken—people crawling up on the top of each other."

Munch was always in a state of conflict with himself. The stronger his yearning to do one thing the more likely he was to do the exact opposite.

During his years of popularity, thousands wanted to befriend him. Artists and patrons felt it a privilege to be admitted to his house, to see him and talk to him. Nevertheless, he felt neglected and forgotten.

Although he could not stand having people around he played his radio day and night to be surrounded by voices. Feeling most relaxed when he was able to be by himself among masses of strangers, he loved railway stations and station restaurants. He liked to travel too —felt drawn toward the unknown. His great shyness served as a protection against his strong craving for tenderness and his great desire for knowledge—just as dizziness protects its victim against the desire to jump. He who suffers from dizziness does not dare climb a steep precipice—he senses the danger, and for him it *is* dangerous because he trembles from the desire to let go.

Thus Munch, who said he could not stand to be with many people at one time, liked to eat in station restaurants and often had dinner at Oslo East Terminal.

"I go down there to look at the ants crawling," he said. "A railway station is like an ant hill—creatures running in and out hardly having time to sit down. They come dragging their parcels and suitcases. I look at them and wonder what they are doing for a living, what they have in their parcels. Only yesterday I saw a young woman put down a big brown parcel—so furtively, I thought. She looked around very cautiously. I noticed she was searching for a particularly good spot to put it down. She did not return to pick it up again. A big brown parcel it was. I don't know how I'm going to be able to paint it—it contained a dead child, I think. Perhaps she had killed it."

Where can a man in a crowd be more by himself than in railway stations and public dining rooms? With people all around, he may still remain a stranger, watch the activities of the others, feel close to them without revealing himself. For the average person tenderness forms a bridge to other human beings. To Edvard Munch tenderness was something treacherous, a trap, a shaft through which he might tumble into an inferno of anguished passion.

It was this Edvard Munch who, seeking refuge behind a mask of shyness and discontent, led his nearest friends to believe that he resented their company and simply wanted to do nothing but paint. Seeing his shyness, his sensitivity, and experiencing his unpredictable moods, they failed to recognize in these traits a deep desire to establish bonds of friendship with all people. If a person stopped Edvard Munch in the street the artist might chat for quite a while, then stop abruptly: "What do you mean by doing this to me? Stopping me on the street like this and going on talking for ever!"

The Norwegian art periodical *Kunst og Kultur* in an issue in the 1930's showed two Munch pictures, one marked by the editor "Before 1905," the other "After 1905." This, somehow, infuriated Munch, and he questioned the editor about it:

"What did you mean by using those dates?"

"To tell the truth, I don't know," the editor replied.

"Rasputin!" Munch shouted.

It was in 1905 that Munch had left Norway temporarily. Being reminded of this by the two pictures, he thought people had started gossiping about his reasons for leaving.

Oslo is not a big city, and it was almost unavoidable that Munch and Gustav Vigeland would run into each other soon or later.

"Well, well. How is the old primadonna?" Vigeland asked when they happened to meet.

"Primadonna?" Munch huffed. "Primadonna, now." He tore off his hat in a grand gesture and replied with pretended humility: "Thank you, quite well, Mr. Wholesaler."

"Wholesaler?"

"Yes," Munch replied, "I understand you are involved in a big business enterprise."

It might be nothing more than pure absentmindedness that made Munch appear brusque and unfriendly. He met Ludvig Karsten one day and invited him for dinner at the Grand Hotel where they were not placed at Munch's usual table. Munch played the genial host, choosing carefully the menu and the wine. Having placed the order he left for the washroom and, when he returned, took his place at his familiar single table and asked for the menu.

Surprised, Karsten came over to him: "Don't you want to have dinner with me?"

"Of course, I do," Munch was all smiles, "with pleasure. When did you get to town?"

One of Munch's friends, really a favorite of his, used to visit him at Ekely every Sunday. One day Munch confided in me:

"How am I supposed to get anything done? I can never paint on Sundays for then Halfdan Rode comes—every blessed Sunday Halfdan Rode comes. Why don't you tell him to call first?"

Shortly thereafter, Halfdan Rode arrived, and Munch refused to let him in. This was not so unusual. Munch often refused to admit people—sometimes even his best friends.

"Is it not convenient that I come in?" Halfdan Rode

Selvportrett foran husveggen på Ekely, 1926
Selfportrait in front of the House at Ekely, 1926
91,5 x 73 cm, Munch-museet, Oslo

Piken og døden, 1893
The Maiden and the Death, 1893
128,5 x 86 cm, Munch-museet, Oslo

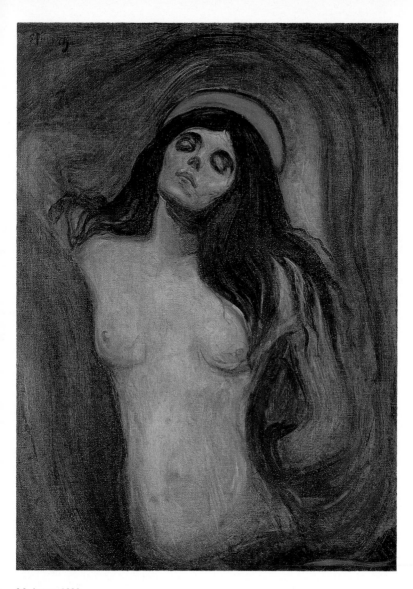

Madonna, 1893
Madonna, 1893
90 x 68,5 cm Munch-museet, Oslo

Stjernenatt. Ekely, 1923-24
Starry Night. Ekely, 1923-24
139,5 x 119 cm, Munch-museet, Oslo

Møte under kastanjen. Hanna Brieschke og Rolf Stenersen, 1937
Meeting under the Chestnut Tree. Hanna Brieschke and Rolf Stenersen, 1937
70 x 60 cm, Munch-museet, Oslo

Selvportrett i parken på Ekely, 1938-42
Selfportrait in the Park at Ekely, 1938-42
60 x 80 cm, Munch-museet, Oslo

Oslo-boheme. Birgitte Prestøe, Rolf Stenersen og Jappe Nilssen, 1926-30
Oslo Bohemians. Birgitte Prestøe, Rolf Stenersen and Jappe Nilssen, 1926-30
72 x 100 cm, Munch-museet, Oslo

Mellom klokken og sengen, 1940-43
Between the Clock and the Bed, 1940-43
149,5 x 120,5 cm, Munch-museet, Oslo

Skrik, 1893
The Scream, 1893
91 x 73,5 cm, Nasjonalgalleriet, Oslo

asked politely as Munch peeked out through the half-opened door.

"No, it's not," he replied curtly, "and it wasn't convenient last time either. In fact, it's never convenient."

Rode left.

"Do you know what Rode said the other day?" Munch asked me. "'You've got nothing to worry about,' Rode said, 'having a millionaire for an errand boy.' Now, what could he possibly have meant by that?"

A while thereafter, he complained about his loneliness.

"No one calls on me anymore," he said. "Not even Halfdan Rode. Why don't you ask him to come? But remember, he must telephone me first."

In the 1930's, Munch selected twelve paintings to be crated and sent to Edinburgh for exhibit. After the crate had been nailed shut, however, he reopened it, removed one canvas, and replaced it with two others. Later, learning that the Edinburgh exhibit included only twelve of his pictures, he paced the floor in great agitation as he commented to me on the news:

"My best picture may have been stolen ... and I didn't even want to take part in the exhibit," he added looking accusingly at me who had suggested that he participate.

When the crate arrived back from Edinburgh Munch insisted on opening it personally. As he pulled out the first canvas he remarked:

"Aha, that one the thief didn't want. It'll be exciting to see what he has chosen. Who knows, it may have been a thief with good taste. If he has taken the largest canvas I'll report it to the police, but if it's the best one he has taken he can keep it. It's possible, isn't it, that a thief can become fond of a picture? I surely don't want to report a poor man who becomes so taken with a picture he simply can't resist stealing it."

There were thirteen canvases in the crate. The thirteenth, a reclining nude, the puritanical Scotsmen had withheld from the exhibit. That no picture had been stolen apparently irritated Munch considerably:

"All a thief wants these days is silverware and money," he muttered angrily. "Thieves are so stupid they don't realize that a single painting can be worth a whole lot more than a crateful of forks!"

"Why don't you go to the movies with me tonight," Munch suggested one day in the 1930's. "It's such a long time since I saw a movie."

We decided to go to the seven o'clock show, but when we got to the theater and he noticed that it was located in the immediate vicinity of the Town Hall which was then under construction he wanted to have a look at that before we entered.

"Everyone should build so that he has a view," Munch said. "And here in Oslo, a city on hills facing the fjord, all streets ought to be laid out in such a way that the fjord and the harbor would always be visible. Now, with this new building, they have closed the view completely. Right here where the Town Hall has been placed we used to catch a glimpse of the sea, but now that's gone. Just think of it—Oslo, the great shipping center, and no glimpse of the sea.

"Well, so that's the Town Hall"—he looked up and down the towering scaffolded structure—"it's pretty. The scaffolding, I mean. I can't tell what it'll be like when they take that down. Wood scaffolding is vivid, in a way —creates a Gothic effect. Of course, to build in Gothic style today is plain dishonesty," he added, as if to emphasize that he had no objection to the simple modernism of the structure before him. "Gothicism is a way of life which no longer applies, a style created by people living in the woods—an index finger pointing to the sky." He grew eloquent: "If you look carefully at the trees along a path in the woods you'll notice that they merge in Gothic arches. The rose window is the sun—the sun low and visible through the trees. That sketch I have painted on my living room door is the sun in the woods —it gives you the feeling of a rose window. The trees

130

along the road I have given crests that merge into Gothic arches."

When we got to our seats in the theater the film had been running for some time.

"Do you understand any of this?" Munch asked. "Is it an English or an American film?"

"It's American."

"American? How do you know the difference? It surely sounds English to me."

"Ssh! Ssh!", we heard round about.

"Is it me they're shushing," Munch asked annoyed. "Let's go and sit somewhere else."

We moved farther toward the back and Munch resumed his whispering. More shushing. We got up and left.

"That shows you what people are like in this city," he complained. "Yesterday someone threw stones onto my property, and last winter I couldn't walk down Hoff Hill without being pursued by sleds.

"'Out of the way!' the children shouted, and I, old and decrepit, had to scramble behind a tree like a squirrel!"

Although Munch himself kept watch dogs that barked furiously at anyone approaching Ekely he sued a neighbor for having a barking dog in the house.

"I have to sneak into my own house," he told me. "My neighbor keeps a German shepherd especially trained to fleck its teeth to errand boys and me."

When Munch called me one evening and asked me to rush out to Ekely I knew from his tone of voice that something unusual had happened. He sounded both angry and depressed.

On my arrival, without saying as much as hello, he approached me with his mouth wide opened and pointed to the empty space from a molar that had been pulled. "Can a dentist pull a tooth without asking his patient's permission?" he asked. "It's incredible, isn't it? Frankly, I can't stand people anymore. They feel they can act in whatever way they please with me."

131

Munch had an aversion for signing his name. Once, having sold a painting for ten thousand *kroner,* he was paid by check and went to the bank to cash it.

"Would you endorse it, please?" the clerk asked.

"Endorse it? What do you mean? Isn't the check any good?"

"Of course, it's good. It's only a formality, Mr. Munch. We can't give you the money without receiving your endorsement. You do it by signing your name on the back."

"Only a formality, heh? When did it become just a formality to place your name on other people's checks? I remember how my father used to struggle to keep up payments on notes he had signed. Is this check any good or isn't it?"

"It's only a formality, Mr. Munch. This type of check requires your endorsement."

Munch picked up the check and walked out—directly to my office.

"You should have seen the furore I created down in the bank," he said. "The bank mob flocked around me —'It's right, Mr. Munch,' they said, 'the check must be endorsed. It's just a formality.'"

It took me quite some time to convince him that the bank clerk had been right. When he got up to leave he said:

"From now on I want no checks. At least, I don't want to go to the bank anymore."

Munch was indecisive about exhibits. He wanted his works shown and he did not. To succeed in getting his permission to arrange an exhibit, one had to approach him at the right moment—on one of the few days when he really wanted to exhibit—and pick up the pictures then and there.

"Why should I, old man that I am, want to exhibit anymore?" he would ask in frustration and annoyance. "Haven't I had enough exhibits? I've no need for it, and I don't get around to paint while the exhibit lasts. All I do is read the reviews—everything they write about me I read. Besides, only the Lord knows what they might be writing. To exhibit is like being called on to recite in school. I really can't take it. Should I fail this time the entire card house might come tumbling down.

"I can't keep showing *Sick Girl* over and over again. The public ought to see some of my new pictures. Perhaps they think I'm done for. Many painters lose their sense of color with age—Gerhard Munthe did and Heyerdahl too. Perhaps it might be good for people to see that these 'mural brothers'"—he was referring to Per Krohg and Alf Rolfsen—"aren't the only ones who paint in this country."

When we took away his pictures he became very uneasy.

"I don't want to sell any of them," he warned anxiously. "Please, remember, I don't want to sell. It'll be so empty around here. All the children are in school—they'll be called on to recite their lessons."

In 1928, while Denmark and Norway had the Greenland dispute pending before the International Court of Justice, Munch's private collection, almost all of it, was being shown in Berlin. I ran into him at "Skansen", the outdoor restaurant above Oslo harbor, where he sat with his nose buried in piles of newspapers—German, French, Danish, and Swedish.

"Congratulations on your great Berlin success," I said.

"Congratulations?" he countered scornfully. "Don't you see I'm just sitting here reading? I do nothing but read. The Lord only knows whether I'll ever paint again. This painting was an illness with me, and now I may have been cured. Yesterday I was going to paint a little when I suddenly decided to take a walk instead. Thereafter I took a bath, ate a steak, and sipped a bottle of champaigne. I was in high spirits and really quite satisfied when I went to bed. Slept like a log. Yes, I may finally have been cured. When I woke up this morning all I could think of was to get down town to buy more newspapers."

He glanced at one or two and pulled out a Danish edition.

"How petty the Danes can be! What the devil do *I* have to do with the Greenland dispute? Not a word about my exhibit in any Danish paper."

One morning—it was the day before Christmas—I called on Munch with some flowers. When I was about to leave he held me back.

"Please, stay a while longer," he pleaded. "I'm so lonely. Everybody thinks I prefer to be by myself, but no one really likes to be lonely. Whom can I call?" He flapped his arms and dropped them to his side. "Jappe Nielsen has passed away—all my friends have passed away. I don't have a single person I can call anymore."

"Why not come home with me? It would be such a pleasure to have you."

"No, no. You've got to take care of the children, go around the Christmas tree and sing. I don't even have a Christmas tree in the house. Why don't you come along down town and help me buy a Christmas tree; then I'll drop you off at your house?"

He called for a taxi and we headed toward town while he chatted amiably about the old days.

By the time the taxi stopped Munch had forgotten the purpose of the trip.

"A Christmas tree, you say? What am I supposed to do with a Christmas tree? Oh yes, that's right, a Christmas tree you said. Is five *kroner* enough?"

He stayed in the taxi while I chose the tree. Thereafter we returned to Ekely where I brought the tree into the house and placed it by the door.

At first he paid no attention to it. Then, all of a sudden, he stopped and stared at it in anger and frustration.

"Did you buy that thing for me?" he blurted out.

"Yes. Is something the matter with it?" I looked bewildered at him, and at the tree. Then it dawned on me: a naked evergreen leaning against the doorpost was a decorative feature reserved for funerals only. Distressed at my momentary thoughtlessness, I picked up the tree and brought it back to the car. Before I had time to turn around and wish him a merry Christmas, Munch had gone into the house and slammed the door behind him.

The Last Years

In his old age, Munch suffered from high blood pressure and dizziness. He walked poorly and with shuffling feet, and, tiring easily, would rest frequently in the course of the day. He slept sporadically—rose early in the morning and retired early at night. He had little appetite and ate only when he felt hungry. Often unable to recall whether he had eaten or not, he would suddenly interrupt a conversation and ask: "Have I had anything to eat while you've been here? I feel so hungry."

Then, without moving from his chair, he would call to his housekeeper: "Are you there? Have I had dinner today? I'm hungry. Would you bring me something?"

But the housekeeper's arrival with a tray might evoke this reaction: "Did I ask for food? I don't want to eat again if I've just finished. Besides, I have a guest."

In 1930, when a blood vessel burst in his best eye, he lost all vision in it. Gradually, however, the eye returned to normal. At the outset, threatened with total blindness, he became almost sick with fear.

"I'd rather lose my arms," he said. "You can be a great painter even though you may not draw or paint well. Look at Goya. Then, on the other hand, there is Zorn, the Swede. His great facility ruined him. He created a totally dead art. Perhaps the loss of an arm might have given him the soul of an artist. At least, he wouldn't have gotten quite as many portraits to do. Everybody wanted to be painted by Zorn. They queued up and were painted on assembly line."

As Munch's eye improved his spirit quickened. In the process of convalescence he had strange visions and saw peculiar colors. These phenomena he has tried to express in a series of drawings and colored sketches which also show the gradual improvement of his sick eye. At first, there seems to be a claw grasping his eye. Later, this changes to a bird.

In 1938, in preparation for a Munch exhibit in Amsterdam, the director of the art collection of the Dutch capital arrived in Oslo. Munch, tired and out of sorts, refused to meet with him. The director demanded to see Munch, however, and the artist consented to step out into the garden of Ekely to greet the visitor there but could not be persuaded to invite him in.

"I'm sorry, but I can't let you in," he apologized. "I haven't made my bed yet. In this house it takes two weeks to clean up." Relenting a little, he added: "I'll let you stand on the threshold and peek in if you'd like, provided you look at the walls and not the floor."

Having gotten no farther than to the artist's threshold, the Dutchman was quite disappointed in the reception and told me so. Consequently, I called Munch the next day and pleaded with him to show the director the courtesy of bidding him good-by, and he promised to meet us in a small restaurant down town.

"Perhaps we should go somewhere else," I suggested to Munch when I discovered how smoke-filled and stuffy the place was.

"No, no. This is like the old days—a homecoming after all the dull years at Ekely."

Later, when I was to accompany the pictures to Amsterdam, Munch gave me final instructions:

"Remember to tell them that no picture is for sale. However, if they make an attractive offer on a special painting you may let them have it as a gift."

The exhibit, though enthusiastically received, did not result in a bid on any picture. I telephoned Munch from Amsterdam:

"Why not give the city a picture anyway?"

"No," he replied glumly. "Besides, this exhibit in Amsterdam was *your* idea. Paris was *my* choice."

The possibility of a Paris exhibit was very much on Edvard Munch's mind in his later years. "I've got to expose myself," he said, "have a major exhibit in Paris."

However, he insisted on an official invitation from the French state and on the use of the exhibit halls in Jeux de Paume. After a series of successful exhibits in Berlin, Zurich, Oslo, Stockholm, and Amsterdam, the long-awaited invitation from France finally arrived, and the French ambassador called on Munch in person. Munch expressed his appreciation but informed the ambassador that he needed some time to prepare the details.

Knowing how much he had looked forward to this opportunity, I gladly assisted him in his preparation, particularly in the selection of canvases. The French ambassador had insisted that Munch write a personal letter of acceptance to the state. In my effort to bring this about, however, I failed completely. Try as I would, I could not prevail on him to comply. The ambassador called Jens Thiis and Thiis in turn called Munch:

"What about that letter to the French state?"

"I don't know," Munch replied indecisively. "I'll have to give it careful consideration—the exhibit, I mean. It's no small matter to exhibit in Paris, you know. There they're not a bit interested in what has been said about my pictures in other countries."

The French, waiting in vain for the letter of acceptance, finally gave up, and the Paris exhibit was never held.

"The devil take Thiis," Munch said later. "He knew perfectly well I never write letters. Perhaps someone whispered something into *your* ears too," he added with a sudden flicker of suspicion; "I know you've been buying some paintings by these 'mural brothers.' Of course, that's none of my business. But, knowing how much that Paris exhibit would have meant for me, couldn't you have helped me out? Remember the London exhibit? Well, all you did was to come up here and pick out the paintings—didn't ask about a thing. No letter was required then." He looked at me, deeply disappointed.

"Was it Thiis, I wonder, or you who ruined this Paris

exhibit ... I never write letters any more, my thoughts wander so much I've found it necessary to stop writing. I can't even read what I'm supposed to sign."

"But I did offer to write the letter for you," I protested.

"Of course you did, but Thiis said it was improper if I didn't write it myself."

Munch sympathized with the working class and had no ambition in the direction of bourgeois riches. Yet he joined no political organization and never cast a vote.

"If I did vote," he said, "I'd vote for *Dagbladet* or *Arbeiderbladet,*" identifying the political parties by their principal dailies, the liberal *Dagbladet* and the Labor Party's *Arbeiderbladet.* "I'm sure I'd never vote for *Aftenposten* or *Morgenbladet,*" he added, referring to the conservative papers.

Of course, the conservative press had been persistently critical of Munch's art.

He liked to keep up on political events and was very much concerned with his own country's state of preparedness. Seeing what happened abroad in the 1930's, he felt that Norway ought to strengthen her defence system and develop an air force.

On a wall in his house in Aasgaardstrand he had tacked up a 1905 newspaper clipping announcing Norway's separation from Sweden. With the years, the clipping turned yellow, but when a cleaning lady wanted to remove it Munch emphatically pointed out its importance:

"Don't touch that!"

"Why not? It's just an old clipping."

"That clipping is from the first paper printed in a totally independent Norway."

On Munch's seventy-fifth birthday Oslo's young people wanted to honor him with a torchlight parade. He refused to cooperate.

"Who's behind this?" he asked. "Søren perhaps? No, I don't want any torchlight parade. Who knows what'll happen? It might rain and no one would turn out."

On the same occasion, Oslo Radio wanted the Norwegian people to hear his voice, and I was asked to be in charge of such a program. Again Munch refused.

"What would they want me to talk about?" he asked when I discussed the matter with him. "I'm no good at things like that."

"They want me to prepare a script," I explained. "I'll be saying something about your pictures, ask questions, and you'll provide the answers."

"You mean, I would have to say what you had already written down? No, thank you; that sort of thing I can't do."

An international clipping service furnished him with articles and reviews about his works. Most of these he read eagerly, even in the 1930's when hardly a day would go by without the publication of some article or other about him. Only rarely did he personally receive representatives of the press.

Many artists wanted to paint his portrait, but he refused to sit for others and instead provided us with a series of penetrating self-portraits.

With ample funds available, he hired one of Oslo's best photographers to take pictures of his paintings as soon as he felt they were completed.

"I should have had an album for all these photographs," he said as he looked through the pile of pictures that had accumulated. "But I can't take time to sit here and paste for hours on end. For a while a janitor was doing it for me, but he soon tired of it."

"You mean, you don't enjoy looking at the pictures?"

"Oh yes, I like to look at pictures, all right. It's the paste I can't stand the sight of!"

Munch was at Ekely when the Germans occupied Oslo on the 9th of April, 1940. In the subsequent weeks there was considerable air activity around the city. German planes seemed to be on the wing around the clock.

"Look," Munch said in exasperation, "it's my house

they're circling. They're doing it to annoy me, to upset my working conditions."

His basic fear those days was that the Germans would confiscate his pictures.

"Why did they come here?" he asked angrily. "They'll live to regret it. It won't be so easy for them to escape. They don't know what happened to Sinclair and his troops, do they?" He was referring to a Scottish mercenary who landed in Norway in the seventeenth century and was killed in his first encounter with the peasantry.

When the city offered space in the Town Hall for safe storage for his pictures he considered the offer very carefully but finally declined. Some time thereafter, two Germans came to his house. Thinking they had come to carry out the long-expected confiscation he called me up immediately and urged me in great secrecy and apprehension to come and help him:

"Hurry up," he pleaded in a low and excited voice. "It'll be the last time you'll be able to see my pictures. They're here now. The locust has landed. You know what I mean, don't you? The Green-clad Horde. They're here now—the Germans, damn it!"

The two unwelcome visitors, having come simply to have a look at Munch and his paintings, asked if they might be of service to him.

"Yes, you certainly may. Please see to it that I be allowed to keep on undisturbed. I can't work when I'm surrounded by people."

The Germans and their Norwegian collaborators—the quislings—exerted considerable effort to gain the support of recognized Norwegian artists in their campaign to Nazify Norway. Though largely unsuccessful, they did line up a few individuals of peripheral significance as well as two figures of primary importance, the novelist and Nobel prizewinner Knut Hamsun, and the noted composer Christian Sinding, both of advanced age.

Edvard Munch, seventy-six years old when the German

occupied Norway, was contacted by a Quisling supporter who asked him to become a member of an "honorary board for the arts" on which he would join Knut Hamsun, Christian Sinding, and—so said the caller—Gustav Vigeland. It was Knut Hamsun's son Tore, a painter, who called on Munch.

"You must accept membership on the board," he pleaded. "My father is begging you—if, for no other reason, at least for the sake of old friendship."

"Old friendship?" Munch asked astonished. "Is your father an old friend of mine?"

"He speaks of you as the greatest painter of Scandinavia."

"Is that so? Does *he* have any of my pictures? That's news to me. Which ones does he have?"

Tore Hamsun blushed. Knut Hamsun had no pictures.

"Perhaps he can't afford to buy any," Munch mocked.

The honorary board for the artists never materialized. Munch was unshakeable.

On his eightieth birthday the quislings wanted to arrange a major retrospective exhibit. Munch did not allow it and asked to be left alone. He wanted nothing to do with Germans or quislings.

His caretaker at Ekely aroused his suspicion.

"I don't trust him," he confided to me. "Last Sunday he said something about the "new order"—that we couldn't keep on in the old way. I'd better get rid of him, I think. I'm not obligated to keep him, am I?"

Everywhere in Norway during the occupation there were posters warning the population against anti-German activities and pointing out the dire consequences of such acts. Munch's reaction was characteristic.

"I did a drawing once," he commented. "It represented a man hunting. Underneath I wrote this phrase: 'Behold the audacity! The wounded stag fights back.'"

Munch knew that Norway soon would be free. He knew that the Germans were retreating rapidly on the Russian front, that Germany slowly but surely was being bombed into total ruin and that giant Anglo-American forces were readied for the final assault. But he did not live to see the end.

In December of 1943, a series of violent explosions shook the Norwegian capital. First, a German ship in the harbor blew up, then tons of explosives on the pier were ignited. There were hundreds of casualties; a few buildings in the immediate harbor area were destroyed, and throughout the city, also at Ekely, windows were shattered.

Munch's housekeeper, thinking the entire city was under attack, insisted that Munch seek shelter in the basement. This he refused to do. Instead, he sat in the stairwell to the basement, thinly clothed, for several hours. As a result, his old bronchitis flared up again, and in the following days he tired easily and lay down frequently.

On longer journeys, he had always taken along a small package of old letters. They were the ones he had received from his aunt, Karen Bjølstad. Now, once more, he read these, the letters written by the person who had done more for him than anyone else. Perhaps he thought how different everything might have been had she entered his life as someone other than his mother's sister.

On the 23rd of January 1944 he was up early and walked around in the main building at Ekely for a while. About two o'clock in the afternoon, feeling poorly, he went to bed, and at six o'clock that evening he passed away, succumbing to a heart attack. He was then a little more than eighty years old.

The sad event took place during the occupation, and the quislings tried to arrange an official funeral. Inger Munch was able to put a stop to that but could not hinder considerable participation by Germans as well as quislings. In the general procession accompanying Munch to his last resting place there was an unusually large number of women.

His urn has been placed in the Court of Honor in the cemetary of Our Savior's Church in Oslo.

Munch's Art

There are three distinctive periods in Munch's creative life. First come the years prior to his inner breakthrough, before his art acquired the characteristics now so definitely associated with him. Although he matured early he was no child prodigy. He was twenty-two years old before he created a masterpiece. Early drawings by Munch indicate that he had learned from well-known masters, from the Norwegian landscape painter Johan Christian Dahl, and, more generally, from Michelangelo. In his mature years Munch cared little for Dahl, but Michelangelo he continued to love throughout his life. In his opinion, the most beautiful artistic creation he had ever seen was Michelangelo's series of frescoes in the Sistine Chapel. Yet it is difficult to detect a direct Michelangelo influence in Munch's mature works.

"I do have this in common with Michelangelo and Rembrandt," he said once, "that the line itself, its rise and fall and the entire curvilinear interplay, always has held greater fascination for me than the color schemes. It's plain to see that the pictures in the Sistine Chapel have been painted by an artist who was first and foremost a sculptor."

In the first period, when Christian Krohg was particularly influential, Munch's canvases are so reminiscent of his teacher's, both in color choice and in brush strokes, that it is sometimes difficult to determine whether they were painted by Munch or Krohg. Occasionally, however, Munch's reflect greater warmth, seem more emotionally motivated.

After his first trip to Paris, he returned home greatly

impressed by what he had seen. To the extent that he was influenced by any particular school, it was the contemporary French that furnished the greatest impetus. Toulouse-Lautrec is undoubtedly the painter from whom Munch learned the most.

The second period in his art encompasses the years before and after the 1902 gunshot in which he lost part of his finger. Starting in 1889, this period lasts until his discharge from Dr. Jacobsen's clinic in 1909, and marks the years of his manhood, the years when he was directly involved with women. His own experiences constitute the core of his art. More than anything else the mysteries of love and death occupy him. The purely pictorial elements —color interplay, surfaces and lines—serve as means to express his undulating moods, his philosophy of life. It was not enough to be a painter—he wanted to be a poet and a thinker as well.

"I know that the big, black sack-like shape in *Puberty* weakens the pictorial element," he confessed. "Yet I had to present it that way, large and monochrome."

Once, speaking about this particular period in his life, he said: "If I had lost my sight, I would have become a philosopher. As it is, I paint. I find it easier than writing and speaking."

Munch's philosophy contained nothing new. It was his opinion that man possessed no free will, that he was only a pawn being moved by a Higher Power.

Human beings are driven together when inner urges issue mating calls—as grains of sand on a copper disc are driven together when a violin bow brushes against the disc. The earth is female—the sun, the moon, the air, and the ocean are male forces embracing the earth and making it fruitful. Every day this takes place and man, like everything living, is a part of this perpetual mating process.

Searching for pictorial means to express this point of view he developed as early as the 1890's a pattern of cubes and squares. The picture *Rendezvous* in *The Frieze of Life* series represents figures—men and women on a beach —painted as broken pieces of cubes.

His philosophy has been particularly beautifully interpreted in the painting entitled *Two People*. A young woman, and, a few steps behind her, a man stand on the shore where earth, sky and sea merge. She looks at the shore and the sea while he looks at her. The horizontal shore line is broken only by these two perpendicular figures. With its simple composition, the picture exudes a mysterious mood—a tension caused by the magnetism that draws the two together. Captivated by the forces of nature they stand in deep anticipation—she not knowing the source of the spirit that flows in her veins; he, waiting restlessly, filled with desire—perhaps hoping that the light of the moon will erase the last vestige of her resistance.

The third and last period in Munch's creative life begins with his discharge from Dr. Jacobsen's clinic in Copenhagen in 1909 and lasts until his death in 1944. No longer oppressed and choked by spiritual problems, sexual drives, and a preoccupation with the morbid, he now becomes a sun worshiper fascinated by color and light. Not only does he revel in these phenomena—it is as if he tries to penetrate the very mystery of their origin, the sunlight itself. Thus, as soon as he has shaken the atmosphere of the clinic he begins to paint the sun, the central picture in the University *Aula* in Oslo. Previously, and when painted by others, the sun on a canvas was no more meaningful than a coin. Munch, painting the sun as it appears on a bright summer day, pictures the primeval source of power and light. Massive, wide clusters of light —yellow, red, and blue—gush forth against the sea and the stony soil and make green plants emerge.

When he resurrects former subject matters, such as *Sick Girl* and *Puberty*, the colors are allowed to glow so intensely that the original psychological content tends to be overshadowed and forgotten. Now it is the master of color and composition who takes over. In the 1920's he painted a new version of an earlier canvas, *The Wedding of the Boheme,* picturing an event from his youth. In the foreground stands a table set for the wedding dinner. However, the bride ingratiates herself with one of the guests with the result that the groom picks up his coat and hat and leaves. Gradually, as Munch worked with the picture, the table became larger and more prominent, the colors brighter and more festive. Finally, the entire painting seems to picture a lavishly laden table, while the dark figures behind it become peripheral. With the table as the center of attention and his friend's unhappiness a secondary concern, Munch has altered the mood of the painting.

In this last period he even starts working on a new frieze, this one with the life of the worker as the principal inspiration—"these gray, exploited masses," he said, "who build our houses, construct our roads, and now very soon will wrest the power from the middle class."

Although he did not get very far with the frieze, he did paint half a dozen brilliant canvases. Most impressive of these is a giant one picturing workers on the way home. They come toward us in dense masses—walk straight on. Anyone trying to halt this slow but powerful human tidal wave will be swept away. Nothing can stop the advance of the workers.

"Do you know who's walking there?" he asked. "It's me, I tell you. The mob has tried to stop me, but it's too late."

In February 1929 he wrote to Dr. Ragner Hoppe in Stockholm:

"I'm well aware of the fact that many here in the Scandinavian countries have been opposed to my approach to painting—its large format and also the way I have tried to treat psychological problems. The new realism with its attention to details, its smooth execution and limited format has penetrated everywhere. It would not surprise me, however, if this type of painting soon will vanish. With its small canvases and large frames it's a bourgeois art intended for living room walls. It's an art dealer's art which rose to prominence after the bourgeois victory in the French Revolution. We live in the era of the workers.

I wonder if art won't become everyone's property again and take its place in public buildings on large wall surfaces."

It's safe to say that Edvard Munch's failure to finish the new frieze was rooted in his lack of inner strength to carry out the particular task at hand. All his life his art had been an expression of his own inner struggle. His solidarity instinct was not strong enough to make his art speak on behalf of society. The decorations of the dining hall in Freia Chocolate Factory bear this out. Painted in 1922, these murals, intended as a hymn of praise to the workers and planned as a set of scenes from their lives, turned out to be beach landscapes and other pictures reminiscent of his earlier paintings.

When asked to take part in the decoration of Oslo's new Town Hall he hesitated giving a definite answer. Wanting to be certain he was equal to the task, he began to lay out a grandiose mural representing workers building the Town Hall. For ten years this unfinished painting faced him at Ekely. Into the canvas he wove pictures he had painted before—he had given up painting anything new. It was as if his original creative power gave way. Incidentally, it is curious that he painted only working men, never working women. These pictures of workers were done during the period in his life when he also often painted male nude studies.

In the 1920's, when a new volume of the Norwegian sagas was in the planning stages, Munch was asked to contribute some illustrations. In preparation he completed a few woodcuts in which he made use of a style generally applicable to saga illustrations; then, claiming that he found it impossible to alter his technique and approach to make his drawings harmonize with those of other illustrators, he decided against participating in the project. Actually, his reason for withdrawing did not lie in any such technical matter. Even in this work *The Frieze of Life* haunted him. Pictures like those of Jappe Nielsen sitting on the Aasgaardstrand shore and the portrait of his friends Christian Gierløff and wife, show up in his proposed saga illustrations, only now his models have been given sword and armor.

Munch always declined invitations to take part in projects he felt uncertain about. No amount of money offered would make him change his mind.

"Why should they want me, an old man, to paint pictures for the Town Hall?" he asked with annoyance. "People would judge my contribution on the basis of those pictures and forget what I painted in the best years of my life."

If the letters Munch wrote to relatives and friends were collected and published they would undoubtedly throw new light on his life and contribution. Even so, the letters would reveal only a fraction of everything his paintings disclose. To get close to Edvard Munch it is necessary to follow him from painting to painting. His letters are by no means as open. When he used words he was always on his guard. Only when he wrote the poem *Alpha and Omega* did he reveal himself as fully as in his pictures.

His letters show that he was plagued by restlessness and doubt in regard to things he had said or done. His handwriting is revealing and reflects the same characteristics that his art does—his loneliness, his sensitivity and fear. It also reflects his desire to break with established rules —and first and last it demonstrates his unique creative talent.

The great space between words in his letters reflects Munch's loneliness. Each word stands alone. All his letters are characterized by great hurry. The handwriting is breathless and staccato-like, the words often split into syllables, an indication of restlessness and fear—a hypersensitive mind. Dots above *i*'s and *j*'s are left out, and he never bothers with commas and periods. He breaks established rules.

His handwriting, barren and simple and devoid of ornamental designs, is closed in and angular, yet marked by even and steady pen pressure. It shows that he was difficult and stubborn—a strong-willed person.

His handwriting never changes. He is always himself—does not write differently or more attractively on the envelope than in the letter.

Often he leaves out word endings, peels off everything but the essential. It is obvious that he tries to arrive at the simplest form of expressing thoughts and feelings.

He never boasts—signs his name entirely without decor or pride. He writes Edvard Munch the same way he would write Hans Hansen.

His great creative talent is revealed in his treatment of the words. No series of common letters, the words stand out as meaningful symbols. And, despite a careless, even ugly, handwriting the total impression of the written matter is one of rare beauty.

His handwriting is rhythmic. The surface of the paper is attractively divided. All written lines form curves, even the sequence of the lines forms a curve. Especially beautiful is the curving on the left side of the sheet. This tends to demonstrate that he would prefer to "stay hidden" over on the side. But then he checks himself and tries to make better use of the available space, thereby reflecting a disciplined approach to space utilization.

It is unlikely that Edvard Munch ever painted or drew an absolutely straight line. Even the roof of a house or a wall would be painted with lines slightly curved. He shunned straight lines. Trees, trunks, or branches are favorite subjects, but pillars and posts are absent. Although he may not have been conscious of it he did feel that only the curved line has beauty and life.

In his own opinion, Edvard Munch was greater as a graphic artist and a creator of black and white drawings than as a painter. "Karsten has learned something from me," he said once; "yet in his best paintings there is something jewel-like in color that I have rarely attained. His colors shine like polished stones. I always liked to see Karsten's exhibits."

His relationship to Karsten, the friend he almost killed, was peculiar. Perhaps he was so fond of him that he *wanted* to admire his paintings. Perhaps it pleased him especially that this great, unemotional painter professed his indebtedness to him.

In the graphic field Munch was truly a magician. In the entire world of art no one has opened as many new vistas in this field as he did, and no one has created as many deeply sensitive and beautiful graphic works. All fit together like pages in a diary in which he describes not the external events of his life but his inner struggle.

Edvard Munch produced approximately eight hundred etchings, woodcuts, and lithographs, most of them rooted in *The Frieze of Life* and describing love, sickness, death, and anxiety. A few represent the world of the workers.

When he liked a painting he would also make a woodcut or a lithograph of it. Only rarely would he make the graphic version first and then the paintings. This proves that practically everything he had to contribute he could have completed in black and white. The painting served as the preliminary study while the graphic work was the final result.

He also found time to try his hand as a sculptor. Shaping his subjects in clay he completed them in bronze. Most of this was done in the years between 1913 and 1930.

Only about one third of Edvard Munch's total production relates to love and sex. Nevertheless, almost all his works seem saturated by stymied or frustrated sexual drives. Even his landscapes bear the imprint of thwarted desire. His life anguish and his overwhelming loneliness, the true sources of his creative strength, penetrate every subject matter. That is why he could produce only one frieze, *The Frieze of Life*.

During the long period from 1889 until 1909 his art reflected a sick mind, if by sick we mean deviation from that which is wholesome and average. By the same token, however, no human being would be declared absolutely healthy if subjected to psychological scrutiny. Moreover, the sickly element present in people of Munch's sensitive fiber is not considered sick by a manifestation of its presence but rather by the degree of its intensity. Thus, it is often through persistent observation of hypersensitive individuals that we arrive at the most profound knowledge of our own inner being. In these individuals we uncover problems we ourselves may be battling in deepest secrecy. Like other great artists Edvard Munch holds up a mirror to us; his pictures provide glimpses of that which moves within ourselves. Munch's art is dominated by thoughts and moods arising from his own inhibitions and difficulties, and it is in his treatment of these psychological elements that he has made his pioneer contribution.

The close relationship between Munch's own psychological characteristics and his approach to painting—his brush strokes and choice of subject matter—is immediately apparent. In the act of painting and drawing he released a flood of personal desires and drives. To him the creative process meant research and description, play and poetry, singing and music, weeping and smiling, confession and rebellion; and first and last love and ecstasy—long curved lines gliding in undulating movements across the canvas revealing his innermost secret desires.

Reluctant to paint "repulsive parts" of the human body he departs from the detailed rendition and instead paints sketchily and in broad lines, thus avoiding calling attention to these features and at the same time being better able to concentrate on the essential theme. By eliminating peripheral matters he forces the viewer to step back to gain distance and scope and thereby discover the totality of the picture; for, after all, beauty is not Munch's primary objective. He has something to convey.

"My pictures must be viewed from a distance," he insisted. "If not, the viewer misses the totality, and my message escapes him. I don't paint leaves and twigs, fingernails and warts."

Yes, Munch's pictures must be viewed either at a distance or in a dimly lit room.

He felt certain that his own problems represented

those of mankind and sought a mode of expression that would emphasize the universal. This he arrived at very quickly. We find it in his sketchily drawn, or even completely hidden faces. His group pictures often tell us simply that we are confronted by man and woman. Had he revealed distinctive facial features he would also have portrayed specific individuals—hard or soft, wise or foolish—and not the subject he really wanted to portray, man and woman.

The contents of Edvard Munch's pictures, often tenuously poised on the threshold between reality and dream, reflect the rich fantasy inherent in this very realm of personal existence and give loftiness and strength to his total creative effort. Yet his pioneer contribution does not lie primarily in this but rather in his ability to give these moods, these thoughts and visions, not only radically new but fully valid artistic expression. There may be painters who have produced pictures equally beautiful and profound, but no one else paved as many new paths. More than any other artist Edvard Munch demonstrated the numeros possibilities present in the juxtaposition of colors and lines and consequently proved that the expressive potential of the painter's art is infinite.

Fleeing from reality, Edvard Munch sought refuge in his art which then ultimately became his only reality. His eyes would glow with pleasure at the successful completion of a work. "I have remained faithful to the Goddess of Art," he said once; "therefore she has not abandoned me."

Because his involvement in art solved his difficulties and released his desire he was able to surrender most of the normal pleasures of life. Behind the Goddess of Art loomed a sacred image, the memory of a woman to whom he remained faithful: his own mother. Having lost her before he had gained the necessary maturity to be freed from her influence, he could never forget her or get over the loss. All his pictures of love, all his female nude studies, point to this. It was possible for him to desire a woman, to admire the beauty of her body, but not to love her.

Her evil nature precluded this. Her beauty was only a flimsy mask hiding her innate vulgarity. She was raw and dangerous, exuding the dread odor of blood and death. The picture called *Marat's Death* has in reality nothing to do with Marat. It is a confessional: the act of love is perilous and repulsive—I must not do it again. It is saturated with horror and death. Painted and repainted, this picture must be rooted in his bitterest childhood memory. The naked woman is he; the man lying dead is both he and his mother.

Something in Edvard Munch's art is very reminiscent of the works of Edgar Allan Poe, the great poet of anxiety who was only a child when his mother died. Nearly everywhere in his writings we detect a longing for her, and throughout his life he felt drawn only to women who reminded him of his mother, of her illness and death. Those who yearn so strongly for the mother concept tend to love and hate more passionately than do others the sun and the sky, the earth and the sea, houses and people —everything reminiscent of our origin, our mother.

Edvard Munch, who derived such scant pleasure from living, who experienced no joy in the company of others, actually loved life with such passion that he finally wanted to be one with his own pictures and thereby live on, to dissolve his own being and still exist. Thus, through these pictures, he hoped to remain for hundreds of years among people, continue to give pleasure and exert influence.

The Fruit of His Labors

Among the items Munch left behind were some fragments of a play he had wanted to write, and a sizeable accumulation of autobiographical notes. *From the City of Free Love* was the projected title of the play. The autobiographical notes, concerning people he had met and important events in his life, had been worked on for many years but rarely shown to anyone. It happened that he would comment on the manuscript, and on one occasion I was even allowed to page through it. However, he did not want me to start reading.

"I have recorded everything," he said. "All hell will break loose when people read it. People are so sensitive, you know. In Paris once, when I was drunk, I sent a postcard to a fellow painter here in Oslo. I had drawn a couple of horns on it and written, 'Here are your new horns.' I guess other saw it too, for I addressed it to him in care of the Grand Hotel.

"'You're a pig,' he said, when I met him later; 'but you're a good painter.'

"'I actually like you quite well,' I replied; 'but you're a terrible painter.'"

In the course of his twenty-seven years at Ekely, Munch never allowed anyone on the second floor of his house. When that section was cleaned and straightened out after his death, it yielded under the dust and dirt more than ten thousand drawings and prints, forty pairs of gloves and mittens, and twelve pairs of pince-nez.

One of his last major works is a self-portrait in which he seems to stand at attention, aged and weary, beside the grandfather clock in his bedroom. It is as if he has risen to a formal meeting with death. The picture on the whole is pale and grim. However, the bedspread has been given a few touches of freshness and color which shine and glow and divert attention from the decrepit man by the clock.

This is the way Edvard Munch wanted it to be. Whatever became of him personally was of little concern as long as his pictures would live. All his thoughts and emotions, the sum total of his life, are in his works.

"I have only these pictures. Without them I am nothing."

The city of Oslo received one thousand and eight paintings from the Munch estate. Initially, the estimated value was four and a half million *kroner*. By 1946, however, this had already quadrupled, and by now the collection is priceless.

The city also received 4,443 drawings and 15,391 prints. There were 378 different lithographs, 188 etchings, and 148 woodcuts. The city was permitted to sell ten copies each of his later graphic works. His sister Inger received one hundred prints and one hundred thousand *kroner*. To his niece he willed forty thousand *kroner* and to needy artists thirty thousand.

Besides his three real estate holdings and a few state bonds, he had a bank account of fifty thousand *kroner*, and a dresser drawer contained ninety thousand in one thousand *kroner* bills. Of his furnishings, only the grandfather clock and a mirror had any monetary value. In the dresser drawer where the money was found were also his Grand Cross for the Order of St. Olav, the French Legion of Honor, and his plain pocket watch attached to a shoe string instead of a chain.

Next to the artist's own collection, which is now in Oslo's new Munch Museum, the National Gallery has the best and most complete collection of Munch pictures: forty paintings and several hundred prints. Besides major works, such as *Sick Girl, Springtime, The Day After,* and

Puberty, the gallery has *Madonna, Ashes, The Shriek, Death in the Sick Room, The Dance of Life, Mother and Daughter on the Shore,* and several wonderful winter landscapes. The collection also includes his brilliant self-portrait from 1906, the caressive picture he painted of his sister Inger, a painting entitled *The Frenchman,* and the portrait of Dr. Jacobsen. All of these were painted before 1910. It was through the efforts of Jens Thiis that the gallery made most of these purchases. A few were gifts from Norwegian collectors. When the industrialist Christian Mustad contributed his impressive Munch collection the National Gallery was able to add a few major works from the artist's later years, among them *Man in the Cabbage Patch* and the self-portrait entitled *In the Spanish Flu.* Of pictures done in water colors or colored pencils the gallery has only very few.

The third largest Munch collection—in actual items the second—is the one donated to Aker municipality in 1936 and now housed at the Student Village in the Oslo suburb of Sogn. It contains thirty paintings, mainly from Munch's later years, and a number of colored prints and water colors, many more than in any other collection, except, of course, that in the Munch Museum. The Aker collection has a total of four hundred prints.

The Rasmus Meyer Collection in Bergen ranks fourth in the number of Munch works. Thereafter would probably come the Thiel Collection in Stockholm. Ernst Thiel, a Nietzsche admirer, purchased the large, curious picture Munch painted of this romantic and misinterpreted poet and thinker. In its curvilinear approach Munch's Nietzsche painting is reminiscent of *The Shriek.* It is as if the landscape in which Nietzsche has been placed twists and twirls around him.

A number of Germans, most of them of Jewish background purchased Munch pictures long before Munch had been able to develop a market in his own country. Among his first patrons were Dr. Max Linde, Max Reinhardt, the publishers Paul and Bruno Cassirer, and the merchant and statesman Walther Rathenau. In Norway, the first Munch collector was the industrialist Olaf Schou, who donated his collection to the National Gallery.

Later, Munch acquired three new patrons in Germany, the Hamburg merchant Arthur Goldstein, a brother of the commercial genius Hugo Stinnes, and the actor Alexander Moissi.

Rathenau, Goldstein, and Stinnes were particularly interested in prints and for many years bought a copy of everything Munch made. Mr. Stinnes' collection was later sold and has been widely distributed.

In Germany and Austria, in a great many collections, are hundreds of Munch paintings and thousands of prints. There are many in Sweden, Denmark, and Switzerland also, while France, Britain, and the United States only have a few paintings and a limited number of prints. Finally, there are Munch paintings in Czechoslovakia, Russia, South Africa, India, and Japan.

While the three largest Munch collections are located in and around Oslo it is unlikely that these will ever be merged. For his own collection, the one he accumulated and protected so diligently, he wanted a separate house.

"If my pictures are displayed in a gallery together with works by other artists they'll be at the mercy of a director or a board," he said; "and who knows what would happen if those people should take a sudden dislike to them. They might be sold, or even worse, thrown into a dark attic. Moreover, I don't want all my pictures under one roof, nor in buildings that are close together. I would worry about fire and air raids. I have no desire to become a myth. Maybe my name would gain by it. Even so, I don't want it that way. I have no children. These pictures are all I have."

Epilogue

In the summer of 1920, a young stock broker sat in a quiet place reading old newspapers. Suddenly, in an issue from the fall of 1918, a few lines caught his attention:

> *To my customers:* The World War is over. There will be no more torpedoing and mass destruction of the world's merchant vessels, but the construction of new ships is proceeding at such speed that the shortage will soon be followed by a surplus. Freight rates, still high, will tumble. Sell your stock while there is still time.
>
> *Karl Meyer.*

He's right, thought the young broker. It's high time to unload shipping stocks. One might even borrow some and sell them. In Norway that was impossible. So he wrote to a Dutch bank and succeeded in borrowing some stocks. These he sold on the Amsterdam Exchange. Within a year he was one of the *nouveaux riches* in a country where wartime profits had melted like snow in the spring.

As a young boy he had dreamed of building huge factories, of producing something useful. First of all, he had wanted to become a composer, but that was impossible.He was the only one in the house who couldn't distinguish between a *b* and a *c*. Then a new Louis Pasteur? That didn't work either, for he failed in foreign languages. A new Henry Ford, maybe? Provide people with better and better goods at continually lower prices. Offer top wages and still scoop in loads of money. Now, at the age of twenty-one he had by luck accumulated one hundred and fifty thousand *kroner*. He felt rich but by no means as happy as he had expected. Somehow, there seemed to be no need for a huge new factory anywhere.

If he wanted to make money he'd have to think of

something else. For him the easiest way was to deal in stocks. As long as new tools and power sources increased the quantity of goods far more rapidly than the quantity of gold, he reasoned, the monetary system based on the gold standard would sooner or later have to disintegrate. In a world saturated with goods and job opportunities, there was certainly a limit to what an average person would tolerate in terms of need and deprivation. As long as the leading statesmen—and all the bankers—comprehended so little of the cause and effect of money that they tied it to something other than the available quantity of goods, it was inevitable that every peak period sooner or later would be followed by a financial crisis. An increase in the quantity of goods required an increase in available money, otherwise the goods would remain unsold. Consequently, statesmen could not simultaneously strive to increase the quantity of goods and keep the quantity of money down. But this, the stock broker realized, was exactly what they were attempting to do. The concept of more work and less expenditures was pure nonsense. He realized too that prices and stocks must fall when governments and people keep saving and that they must rise when the crisis developed to the point that people lost interest in bank accounts and money and desired only goods and real estate. The greater the lack of confidence in money, the more active the stock market. This view of financial affairs was the basis for his trading on the market, and the result was as he had anticipated, except that everything happened so much more slowly than he had thought it would.

He did not agree with those who claimed that the world was governed by crooks, but he was, on the other hand, fairly convinced that those in charge, when it came to monetary matters, were shockingly ignorant and stupid. They "saved" money and wasted the rich supply of goods.

The stock broker realized that he himself was making his money by taking advantage of an error in the economic system. Therefore, as money came streaming in, he began to lose some of the joy of his accomplishment. Ultimately, he shortened his office hours and looked about for a more pleasant and useful way in which to spend his time.

The only solution, it seemed, was to give away his money. Still, that wasn't exactly what he had had in mind. He'd rather find his way to something better.

His first "great gift" was a painting by Fritz Thaulow. The price was 2,100 *kroner*. That was in 1918. He was nineteen years old and had 4,600 *kroner* to his name. It was meant to be the great gift for his parents' silver wedding anniversary. But they thought it foolish to have paid that much for a picture and didn't find it particularly pretty, either. He went to his room and wept. The next day he visited art galleries, finding the price tags as fascinating as the pictures. Had he bought a poor picture? Paid too much for it? In short, had he actually made a fool of himself? Thereafter, visits to art galleries became a daily habit.

Picture buying became a solution. By acquiring an art collection he became an art collector—tied to art. Not an artist, to be sure, but an art lover and a connoisseur. Moreover, he was not handing out money. He might even be able to *make* money that way. Good pictures rose in value.

Yes indeed, buying pictures was a solution. He filled his father's house with pictures. On the walls were "his" pictures. Guests who had listened to his brothers' play the piano, soon preferred to look at his pictures. Nineteen years old he acquired his first Munch works, two nude studies. His father, who published hymn books, found one of them a bit too naked. Still, since the boy had paid so much for it he was allowed to keep it on the wall—with a piece of cardboard covering the bare breasts! It wasn't long before the purchase of Munch pictures gave him the greatest pleasure. He could look at them so often without tiring of them. They were like a book one might read over and over again. It was difficult to place pictures by Munch next to works by other artists. Nothing captivated the eyes as Munch's works did. Moreover, when he saw Munch's pictures he felt a strong desire to write. He might have gone directly from the viewing of such a picture to his desk. This never happened when he saw works by other artists.

In the fall of 1921 he decided to purchase a larger Munch canvas, a major work. There were few available commercially, and the prices were high. Why not try Munch personally? The art dealer said, "Munch receives no one. If you call on him he'll simply say he has nothing to sell."

Even so, he made a trip to Ekely. He rang the door bell and a maid opened up, asking if he was delivering a package.

"I'd like to see Mr. Munch. It's about a picture I'd like to buy."

She disappeared and did not show up again. He pushed the door bell again. At long last, a man came, eyeing him from the threshold.

"Are you Mr. Munch? I'd like very much to buy a picture. I have two. Two nude studies—and eighteen of your graphic works."

"Is that so. Which ones do you have?"

The stock broker told him.

"And now you want to buy more. Do you have any money? You're just a young lad."

"It's money I have earned on my own."

"Where do you work?"

"I've earned it on the stock market."

"Is it possible to make money on stocks these days? I keep hearing that everybody is losing money."

"I have made some. I borrowed some shipping stocks and sold them when they seemed to reach their peak."

"You borrowed stocks?"

"It's all taken care of now. I bought them when they hit their low."

"Is that so? That can be done—sell stocks you've borrowed. How much did you make on it? Yes, I'll let you in. You must leave very shortly. I've heard about you. You offered 1,800 *kroner* for two pictures I had priced at 2,400. You got them at 1,800. I was told you were so young."

As Munch brought him into the living room, the stock broker's eyes fell on the artist's own version of the painting *Kiss*. It excited him—that was the picture he wanted. That, and no other!

"Is that painting for sale? I'd really like to buy it."

"Won't you have a chair? A glass of wine, perhaps?"

"No, thank you. I'm an abstainer. Would you sell that painting for 5,000 *kroner?*"

"Please, sit down. Would you like a cigarette?"

"No, thank you. I don't smoke. I'm in training—going out for track. I'm a runner. Wouldn't you please let me buy that painting?"

"So you're a track man. When I was young we took a drink when we wanted to speed up the circulation. I guess I'm a runner of sorts too. The brief moments I paint I'm a runner."

"Would you sell the picture for 10,000?"

Munch looked at him.

"Twelve?"

Munch didn't answer.

"It's the best picture I've ever seen."

"So you've made your money on the stock market. You're a gambler? I never gamble."

"Please, let me have that picture for 14,000 *kroner!*"

"I suppose you've got to be pretty good in arithmetic to be a successful gambler? Arithmetic was my best subject, but my nerves aren't suited for business transactions. Aren't you afraid things will go wrong? To play the stock market. It must be exciting. And with money you've made on stocks you want to buy pictures. You consider it an investment then, I suppose. You know, during the war people bought like crazy, but this year I've hardly sold anything. To tell the truth, you're the only one who has offered me ten thousand for a picture this year. Last year I received both twenty and thirty thousand."

"Right now fourteen thousand is all I have available."

"No, it's not the price. It's part of *The Frieze of Life*. Ten thousand this year may be just as much as twenty thousand last year. Isn't it so that everything has become much less expensive?"

"Yes, that's the way one has to figure it. Money is merely a means of exchange."

"Maybe you could help me a little. I have some money in various banks, and then this property."

"Bank accounts are all right in periods of depression, when prices of goods decline, but real estate, especially in urban areas, is far better in the long run. What banks do you have your money in? If this crisis lasts I believe many banks will close. If you have money in many banks I'd withdraw it and place it all in the Bank of Norway. You'll get no interest, but your money is safe."

Munch did have his money in many small banks. He withdrew it. Some of the banks later found it necessary to close. Finally, the stock broker advised Munch to withdraw his money from one of the biggest banks of the country. On a Saturday Munch followed his advice. The following Monday the bank closed momentarily. The newspapers wrote column after column about it, claiming it was caused by a rush on the part of the depositors. Tuesday the bank opened again, but Monday Munch caught sight of the stock broker at an exhibit and called to him across the room:

"Thanks for your advice. Yesterday I withdrew my money from ..." and he named the bank.

Many turned around and looked at the youthful expert.

Gradually, the young broker became Munch's financial adviser.

Munch refused to sell the painting *Kiss*. When he bemoaned that no one had given him any specific tasks once the university decorations had been finished, the broker countered:

"How about decorating my father's dining room?"

"How big is it?"

"Twenty by fourteen feet."

"Not very big, but I'll be glad to do it."

During Christmas of 1921 Munch painted new versions of *The Dance of Life, Kiss,* and *Meeting,* charging only

14,000 *kroner* for the lot. The broker's father thought it was too much to pay for pictures. Seeing Munch in the street one day, he went over to him:

"Aren't you the painter Edvard Munch? I have a son who is cracked when it comes to pictures. Right now he's buying only yours. Otherwise he's such a fine, intelligent boy. It seems to me he's investing everything he has in your pictures."

"Your son reminds me of a young German painter I met in Berlin," Munch said. "He followed me from place to place, and when he saw my exhibit in Prague he shot himself."

Munch's goodwill toward the young stock broker was further established by that conversation.

Munch invited him to his home. One Sunday when he came out to Ekely Munch was in the garden with an art dealer. 'I'd better come back later,' he thought and turned around.

"Hey you, Young Norway, are you leaving? Didn't you come to see me? Please, come on in. Do you two know each other? Does the art dealer know Young Norway? He neither drinks nor smokes but is the Norwegian champion runner and makes money on stocks—money he spends on my pictures. That's the way to do it, isn't it? Close your shop and become a track man!"

"I'm glad you came," said Munch after the dealer had left. "That man is such a nuisance. Now he has a customer who wants a winter landscape three feet square. 'Is that so?' I said. 'Too bad. Just now I'm out of winter landscapes three feet square.'"

Munch showed the broker around inside. In one of the rooms was a winter landscape from Hvitsten—three feet square. A landscape featuring some birds.

"It's a good picture," said the broker. "You ought to get quite a bit for it."

"Take it," said Munch. "You may have it as a gift. The art dealer would only get upset if he happened to see it. Those birds are turkeys. I left out the combs. It wouldn't be right to add more red to the picture."

A few years later when the broker had made more money he asked Munch to paint his portrait.

"You're just a young lad," said Munch. "I'd be glad to paint you a few years from now. When you've acquired some features. If I paint you now it'll be nothing more than a picture of a young man—a boy who neither smokes nor drinks. A track man."

Some people were invited to the Royal Palace. *He* was invited to the home of Norway's greatest painter. He did everything to make himself useful. It was important to see to it that Munch didn't tire of him. He knew he mustn't bother him. So he would go to Munch's house only when he was asked to come. It was important too that he chose his conversational subjects with care. Preferably, he should call on Munch when he had something pleasant or useful to report. The most difficult thing was to sit still and stare at the floor while Munch talked. For he wasn't supposed to look at Munch, nor let his eyes wander. He must not offer to buy pictures Munch didn't want to sell. That was considered pressure. Munch didn't like to sell pictures he was especially fond of, but he might *give* them away. Soon the broker preferred only the pictures Munch liked. And when Munch saw him linger at one in particular he might say, "No, no, you aren't going to take that one too, are you? You know I don't want to sell any more pictures." Sometimes he'd have to put the money right into Munchs pocket. "Ugh, do I really have to sell! You must give me a little time." Then he would pick out two or three pictures the broker had to choose among. If he picked one quickly, without hesitation, Munch might say, "Well, that was good of you. It's a poor choice in my opinion—and in yours too. All right, you may bring out your great love. She's right behind the door. She must have noticed your hungry eyes. Seems to put on quite a show when you look at her. I've noticed. Well, it's a gift."

There were many little tasks Munch could assign him. Hire a maid or a watchman. Take care of bills. Find out which of Munch's pictures were available on the market, where they came from and how much the seller was asking. Bid on all pictures for sale to alleviate Munch's fear that one of his works might bring too little. When Munch had gone to Aasgaardstrand or Hvitsten and stood outside his property without a key, the broker would have to drive down with it. He would inform newspaper people when the artist had something he wanted to make known. Help him with his income tax return. Arrange exhibits and sales. Always be available when Munch sent for him. Sit quietly and listen when Munch wanted to talk, and equally important, get up quickly when Munch's flow of words ceased. Munch didn't like to have to ask anyone to leave. Rather, the visitor should say,

"I'd better be going."

Then he'd agree, "Yes, I suppose you'll have to go home. Call me if something comes up."

When he wanted a guest to leave Munch might simply get up and walk away, into the next room. He wouldn't close the door but merely sit there quiet as a mouse. If one happened to look in on him he'd appear drawn and out of sorts, but he'd get up immediately, apologizing,

"You must excuse me. I've been sleeping so poorly."

When Munch needed a new maid he'd ask the broker to help him find a good one. She was not to be younger than thirty and had to be from the country. "I want no art talk. Make sure she doesn't paint or keep running to exhibits. What I want is someone to look after the house and take care of pots and pans." The broker found four or five who seemed suitable. Then Munch came down to the office to pick the one he preferred. At one time he was expected between two and three o'clock in the afternoon but didn't show up until a quarter to four when all the candidates had left. (Each was paid ten *kroner* for their time.) The only person in the reception room was an old, well-to-do lady, one of the broker's major customers. Munch stepped into the room, looked her

167

over and remarked, "You must be way past sixty. How could you possibly think of filling such a post? Are you from the country? I've said I want someone from the country. Why don't you try an old folks' home? You ought to be able to be accepted in some old folks' home or other."

The lady got up, walked out slamming the door. Munch entered the broker's office and said,

"She must have gotten angry!"

The broker knew he could not take his friendship with Munch for granted. He had to take pride in being both errand boy and consultant. By doing such small services for Munch he was allowed to come to his house, see his pictures and listen to his talk. He had to buy the pictures the artist wanted to sell him and accept as gifts those Munch offered. Munch carried on the conversation. The broker was careful not to talk about anything except what Munch wanted to know.

Having sat still listening to Munch's monologues, the broker might get up enough courage to speak:

"Please, listen to me. There's something I must say. It's about the monetary system. Why is it impossible to get people to comprehend that the standard of living would rise instantly if governmental authorities would see to it that the quantity of money increased in proportion to the quantity of goods?"

"What does that have to do with my pictures? Haven't I said I don't understand anything about money? Talk to the professionals."

"Professionals! Only a few of them seem to realize that money is only a means of exchange. Most of them say, 'Have you read Marshall? And Keynes, of course.' We don't become richer by printing money. Remember the trust. What'll happen to the public trust if we keep printing money and the state spends more than it earns?"

"Now, listen! I've told you I don't understand such things."

"Well, that's why we have wars. People don't want to be bothered. They're just as happy leaving it to a few hundred professionals. When I read something by Niels Bohr or Albert Einstein concerning time and velocity I don't understand it, can't follow their reasoning. Even so, I feel that what I read is something grand, my eyes become misty. It's as if I walk in a dark street and suddenly catch sight of the starry sky. But my eyes don't become misty when I read social economics or proclamations from the joint board of the banks. I feel chilled. It's as if they want to rob me of my eyes. Am I the one who can't see the connection or is it the bankers? Is it really possible that these professionals can't see as clearly as I do what constitutes money and what constitutes riches? We live on *things*. That's part of the joy I get out of these stock transactions. When finally everything turns out as I have predicted I feel as if I am able to see something that's hidden to others. I sleep like a log. I know that sooner or later I'll be proved right. It's something I see! If governmental authorities begin now to economize we'll be headed for a new crisis. Of course it pays a society to put everyone to work. A *man* can become rich by saving. A society cannot! On the contrary. A society can "save" itself into poverty. To society paper money is only a means of exchange. Society is rich when it's filled with all sorts of *things*. With rich people it's the opposite. They're rich only when they have what average people are lacking. People often become rich through the exploitation of the shortage of goods. They may own some poor, old houses worth a lot of money simply because there's such a shortage of houses. My God, what a mistake to count a nation's riches in terms of the sum total of what people own in *Kroner!* All right, I won't bother you. You'd rather think of something else and have a war."

"A war? Did you say I wanted war?"

"All I said is that there are all too few who bother to think what this situation with the money and the social household involves. It simply doesn't work to let a couple of hundred bright scholars take care of such important matters. They're practically blind! And their writings! So dull no one can stand to read them. A wilderness of foreign words. Norwegian isn't elegant enough. After all, those who have gone no further than through grade school might understand it! Such writings are so complicated and dry I keep wondering whether those who put them together could ever produce children. I insist that our poverty is the result of shortcomings in our monetary system. 'Money,' they say, and imply riches. 'Riches,' they say, and imply money. That people are short of food is to the advantage of the farmer—if people have money enough to buy. It's the same with everything else. It's the shortage itself that creates the monetary value. Our banks are secure only when there's a shortage of real estate and goods. Most of their money is invested in mortgages and monetary obligations. As soon as there's an adequate supply of real estate and goods, prices drop and with them the monetary value of the mortgages. Nationalization of the banking system is an urgent matter. Far more important than the nationalization of industry. Please listen to me. I have a message. The world is rich, man is thirsty and poor. There's sufficient usable land for everyone now living. Only a fraction is being fertilized and put to use. The earth can feed ten times as many people as it does now. Did you know that? In the crust of the earth there are miles and miles of coal. Thousands of pounds for each one of us. And from two pounds of coal it's possible to generate more power than twenty men can produce. In America there are already forty such "power slaves" behind every human being. Very soon each one of us can have thirty or forty power slaves to do all the rough work. Only, we must see to it that we extract all the riches from the crust of the earth. There's more than enough for all of us. Let's outlaw idleness. Get all the unemployed started. I don't give a damn about the national budget! What kind of nonsense is it that a nation can't spend more than it earns? The quantity of money must rise with the quantity of goods. It's on the consumer side that the Government must step in. To help us buy."

"No, I can't stand it anymore," lamented Munch. "Please, stop, I can't stand it."

Suddenly, looking beyond the broker,

"Do you know what Jappe Nilssen said when I showed him that picture? The one with the rifle? The situation with Karsten which might have ended so tragically? 'Is it from Aasgaardstrand?' he said."

The relationship between Munch and the broker didn't always run smoothly. Now and then Munch said something like this:

"I know you've such good intentions. Still, each has to take care of his own. You your things and I mine. This can't keep on. I don't know how you've slid in here. I haven't ask you to come. You interfere in my affairs. Now it has even gone so far that I learn from a newspaper that I'm going to have an exhibit. I am the only one who doesn't know it."

A few days later the telephone might ring,

"This is Munch. I can't find the right keys. Please drive out here."

When the broker had purchased a painting by another artist he would show it to Munch. If Munch liked it he would praise the broker. If he didn't he would become silent. He wanted the broker to buy pictures by young, "wild" artists. Inquiring about the price, he would complain if he thought it too low.

"Stay away from pictures by dead artists," he said. "Let others buy the "old masters." That's not for you. Don't buy pictures because others like them or because you might acquire a well-known name cheaply. To my mind that's the worst thing you could do. Still, a poor picture by a great artist does give me a good deal more than one a lesser painter has been lucky with. Somehow you always see the mark. There's something in the total approach which tends to captivate. Even so, you should rather buy few pictures and only by those who try to be pioneers. Pictures with content. There's nothing worse than a poor collection of pictures by great masters. Don't listen to what others say. A collection must have direction. It must be a man's opus."

In the 1930's the broker had come across a very early Munch work, a sketch for the major painting *Springtime*. Unsigned, it was not very expensive, so he brought it to Munch in apprehension. Right away, there seemed to be something wrong with it. Munch sat down in a chair and looked critically at the picture.

"You really think I've painted that? Do you like it? Have you bought it for your collection? How much did you pay for it?"

"I believe it's a study for *Springtime*. I paid 1,200 *kroner*."

Munch got up, turned his back to the broker and, stooped over, moved toward the door into the bedroom. He said nothing, did not look back, waved his arms a little. Lifted them only to drop them limply to his thighs. Somewhere in the bedroom he sat down. The broker, silent for a long time, said,

"Would you let me give it to you? Then it'll be out of the world. You've given me so much!"

Munch came back. Went over to the picture, looked at it once more. Then he flung it against the wall.

The broker left. He hadn't gotten very far before Munch came running after him:

"It's your picture. You bought it, paid 1,200 *kroner* for it. I tell you, it's yours. Go in there and pick it up."

He did and for weeks heard nothing from Munch. One day he met Jens Thiis and showed him the picture. Thiis liked it. Said it was wonderful. The broker asked Thiis to give Munch a call and tell him he liked the picture. The next day the broker's telephone rang:

"This is Munch. Thiis called and told me the picture was wonderful. Would you bring it out. I'd like to have another look at it."

Munch settled back comfortably in his chair and scanned the picture for a long time. Then, staring at the broker,

"Answer me now. Do you really think this is a good picture?"

The broker, ill at ease, hesistantly, "It came so cheaply."

Munch got up.

"Won't you sit down," he said. "Sit here. I'm going to get a brush and sign the picture. That'll make it go up in value, won't it? But please don't do anything like that again. I thought you had lost your mind."

Munch signed the picture making the broker feel he was once more back in the artist's good graces. But pity Jens Thiis!

A summer evening in 1938 the broker drove Munch down to Aasgaardstrand. He entered Munch's ugly little cabin where everything was grimy and dark. It was painful to be in there, so the broker dragged the pictures Munch had standing around out into the garden. Then he sat there in the wilderness among the pictures and refused to go inside. Munch roamed around in the house, obviously very much at home. But at long last he stepped outside.

"Come on, let's take a walk and look at all my pictures."

They went down to the seaside and Munch showed him the bridge, the Kjøsterud House with its huge elm trees, the shore with the boulders and little white bath houses.

"As you see," he said, "it's all here. Only people change. Wonder if the old woman is still here, the one who used to think I pilfered her eggs. She claimed I did it by strewing grain from her house over to my garden. The chickens would follow the grain and lay their eggs on my property. When Karsten heard of it he bought some grain and did what she had suspected. We got no eggs, but Karsten painted the chickens—literally, I mean. The old woman came running.

"'They seemed so plain,' said Karsten. 'I thought they needed to be spruced up a little. It's a gift. As a rule I charge fifty *kroner*.'

"Karsten was terrible. Have you heard the one about the lady who approached him about a picture? Her husband wanted a Karsten painting for his fiftieth birthday. When Karsten showed her his pictures she found each one worse than the other. He picked out a large one, placed it across a chair, and said:

'How about that one, mam? Wouldn't that be suitable?'

"Now Karsten had the bad habit of sewing together two canvases. Almost every other picture was sewn together—often with canvases of different texture. The lady approached the painting and let her hand glide along the seam:

"'But it's sewn together,' she said.

"'Is that so?'

"'Of course it is. Here's the seam.'

"Karsten came over. With his finger moving along the seam he said:

"'You're right, mam. It's sewn together. What an unusually sharp eye the lady has for contemporary art.' He helped her with her coat, bowed and said:

"'Greet your husband, mam, and tell him that now, after I've had the pleasure of meeting his wife, I feel sincerely sorry for him.'

"Karsten ... he annoyed me too. We sat in my cabin here in Aasgaardstrand, drinking. I became tired and asked him to leave. But he didn't want to leave.

"'I'd better stay,' he said.

"'Go!' I said.

"'You'll only be hearing things,' he said.

"I had to throw him down the stairs. He held on and we struggled. He didn't do very well. I've made a picture of it. Would you believe it? Karsten went into the garden, attached a thread to the window frame, and stood behind the bushes rubbing the thread with rosin, making it howl more than I could stand. So I got my rifle. I saw the white figure in the semi-darkness. Sure, I'd been drinking a little too. Poor Karsten. You know he fell down a flight of stairs in Paris and broke his neck. Olaf Bull, the poet, and the journalist Bjarne Eide took part in the funeral. Afterward they stopped in a bistro. Olaf Bull lifted his glass and said:

"'Of the blessed departed one may say with absolute truth that he had nothing but enemies.'

"Well, that's not such a bad epitaph! There are plenty of people who climb the social ladder by capturing friends. Oh, they're so sweet, so lovable. If you venture to say they're climbing they'll first become silent, then the words come flowing. Imagine believing such a thing about them. No-no, they had never given that a thought, never for a moment imagined that such a method would pay off. To claim that they had tried to become appreciated and attain power through friends would be an insult to God. They say it as if quoting the Bible: Go out and make all people your friends! Karsten was far too good for that sort of thing. He drank a little and painted a little. Perhaps the drinking helped him paint. That's the way I see it. Remember the big canvas with the fried egg? Yards and yards of huge globs then a black frying pan with a single fried egg. Have you ever seen anything more beautiful than that fried egg? I've been frying eggs myself, but I've never seen anything quite as beautiful as Karsten's egg. But other people are so good, you know. They neither drink nor ever say anything except what people like to hear. They forget that Karsten was a painter. Do you remember that egg?"

When they returned to the cabin Munch lay down. The broker looked for a blanket but didn't find any, so he covered the old man with a raincoat. When he was about to leave Munch said:

"Couldn't you stay here tonight?"

The broker told him he couldn't stand the dark rooms, that he'd rather take a room at the Grand Hotel and look around a little.

"Well-well, now it's your turn to be young."

Hearing music from a dance band, the broker followed the sound. He hadn't been to Aasgaardstrand before. It was at the Grand Hotel they were dancing, so he decided to take a room there and went down to watch the dance.

There was a beautiful girl on the dance floor. She had such a nice laugh. Bjørg they called her. He approached her but caught sight of her legs and changed his mind. He turned around and went back to his room. Damn it! Why did she have to have legs like that? Aasgaardstrand was no place to spend a night. He had seen the pictures, and Munch's cabin was really too awful. He couldn't lie around on the beach either—didn't like to watch drifting clouds and listen to buzzing insects. He couldn't stand to have the sun in his eyes nor burning on his back. He didn't like to lie in the shade either. Shadows, grass, cold water—terrible things. Most people had five senses. He had just about one only. On second thought, he did have two—his eyes and his skin. It was as if he merged with whatever he touched. It was terrible to shake hands with certain people. Munch thought so too. "No, I don't want him out here," he would say, "he always wants to shake hands." Munch too was unable to follow what people said when they spoke in such a way that it evoked pictures. He would hear the first words only. The remainder was only a blurred noise—until an image arose. Perhaps Munch too had sensitive skin. He'd never touch things he didn't like. That's why he became a painter. He had only two sharp senses: everything he saw penetrated deeply, and he liked the feel of the round, even brush. The broker was sorry now he hadn't stayed with Munch. It fascinated him to see how people undress, how they fold their clothes. Hear how they say good night. Most people are apprehensive and say it strangely.

In 1931 the broker published a little book—short fables and sketches. Many had been inspired by Munch's pictures. He had tried to write as he had heard Munch speak—clustered, vividly. Leaps and bounds in time and thoughts. Munch liked the pieces most closely related to his own pictures.

"We have certain things in common," he observed. "I don't care for landscapes either. I'd just as soon paint corpses. Perhaps you'll be writing about me. In fact, perhaps you *ought* to write about me. But not yet, please. I can't have you running around here with a pencil. You ought to read what I have written. I never seem to be able to finish it. All I have time for is this ever-lasting painting. It doesn't surprise me that you are writing. Remember the picture I painted of you back in 1925? The big one I have kept? I painted you as a poet. Come along and have a look."

They went in to look at the picture. Afterwards, Munch showed him another, a portrait of a lady.

"Can you see that she is crazy? Just a few months after I finished the picture she was committed. Everyone thought she was perfectly sane when she posed for me. Even so, I painted her that way."

The broker published a couple of other books and sent copies to Munch.

"Does that new book of yours have anything to do with my pictures? My eyes are getting weak. I can't read much in one sitting. All I can do is page through a book. Do you know Arnulf Øverland? Among the poets he's the best. Olaf Bull is all right too. Well, so you've written another book. Imagine that you who deal in all these important business matters also love pictures—that you always have time to look at pictures! Is it while you are eating that you have your visions and dreams? You're not running anymore but writing instead. Is it something you decide on your own, whether a certain stock will rise or fall? Ernst Thiel carried on that way too. Watch out. You know what happened to him, don't you? More and more pictures and finally no bank."

In the period 1922 until 1942 the broker was the person most frequently invited to Ekely. Months might go without a word. Then all of a sudden Munch might call him as often as eight times a day. The most exciting time to come was when Munch had just completed a painting he was pleased with.

"Perhaps I have learned enough by this time to go ahead and paint the major works I've always been planning to do. My pictures so far are all preliminary studies. My best pictures are the ones I'm going to paint. If I could only have some peace and quiet! Many painters have done their best in their old age. My sense of color has not failed me. I'm not painting yellows and greens the way certain oldsters keep doing it."

Once Munch suggested that there ought to be one great exhibit of his work at which time all pictures would be photographed. The prints too should be stamped and catalogued.

"Maybe I ought to get some people together to organize this. Couldn't you help me out? The Lord only knows what my name will depend on, once I'm gone. See to it, will you, that no pictures are stamped and catalogued unless you're certain they're mine. It's not enough that people insist they have bought them from me. Watch out that my collection doesn't get spoiled by poor sketches and pictures. Of course, sketches are all right, provided they say something. They must be good. Remember, I have only these pictures."

A CHRONOLOGY OF IMPORTANT EVENTS IN THE LIFE OF EDVARD MUNCH

1863.   December 12. Born in Løten, eighty miles north of Oslo.

1882—83. Attended Christian Krohg's Art School in Oslo.

1883.   His first exhibit. Represented at the state-sponsored Autumn Exhibit.

1885.   His first trip abroad during which he spent three weeks in Paris.

1886.   The year of his artistic breakthrough. First versions of *The Day Thereafter, Puberty,* and *The Sick Girl,* the latter painted in 1885 and lost in a fire.

1889.   His first visit to Aasgaardstrand. His first one-man show in Oslo. Recipient of the State Artist's Annuity. Spent four months at the Art School of Léon Bonnat in Paris.

1890.   His first trip to Germany and Italy. Visited France again. Sick with rheumatic fever in Nice.

1892.   Exhibits in Oslo and Berlin and elsewhere in Germany. Met August Strindberg, Dagny Juell Przybyszewsky, and her husband, the Polish poet Stanislaus Przybyszewsky. Met Albert Kollmann. Beginning of *The Frieze of Life* concept.

1894.   A book on Edvard Munch by Przybyszewsky, Meier-Graefe, Willy Pastor, and Frantz Servaes. His first etchings.

1895.   His first lithographs and woodcuts.

1896—97. Lives in Paris. Exhibits in Salon des Independants, Paris, and at Keller & Reinen in Berlin (1897).

1899. The National Gallery in Oslo purchases *Springtime* for 2,500.00 *kroner*. First versions of *Girls on the Bridge in Aasgaardstrand* and *Woman in Three Stages.*

1900—07. Resides for the most part in Germany in the winter and in Aasgaardstrand in the spring and summer. Meets Dr. Max Linde, Count Harry Kessler, Elisabeth Förster-Nietzsche, Max Reinhardt, and Walther Rathenau. In 1902 loses part of a finger. In 1904 exhibits in Copenhagen. In 1906 meets the banker Ernst Thiel of Stockholm.

1908—09. At Dr. Jacobsen's psychiatric clinic in Copenhagen.

1910—15. Resides at Kragerø on the coast of South Norway. Paints the murals for the University Festival Hall.

1911. Purchases the property "Ramme" in Hvitsten at the Oslofjord.

1913—14. Resides at Jeløya in the Oslofjord region.

1916. Purchases the property "Ekely" near Oslo.

1920—22. Journey to Berlin, Paris, and to Italy. Murals for the refectory in the Freia Chocolate Factory in Oslo (1922), and exhibit in Zurich (1922).

1923. Exhibits in the Academy in Berlin and in Gothenburg, Sweden.

1927. Major exhibits in the National Galleries in Berlin and Oslo.

1937. Major exhibit in the General Society of Art in Stockholm.

1938. Major exhibit in the Municipal Art Gallery of Amsterdam.

1944. January 23. Succumbed to a heart attack.

Index